A LITERARY COCKTAIL PARTY

Favorite Drinks from Our Favorite Writers

COCKTAILS AND STORIES BY
KAREN ABBOTT * LOUIS BAYARD * BILL CLEGG *
NOVELLA CARPENTER * SLOANE CROSLEY * MEGHAN DAUM *
JULIA GLASS * LAUREN GROFF * DANIEL HANDLER *
HOMER HICKAM * JOSHILYN JACKSON * A.S. KING *
MIN JIN LEE * EDAN LEPUCKI * SAMUEL LIGON *
BETH LISICK * JACQUELINE LUCKETT * ANTHONY MARRA *
WENDY MASS * VIET THANH NGUYEN * BRAD PARKS *
JAMES PATTERSON * MOLLY PRENTISS * KATE SCHATZ *
AMY STEWART * EMMA STRAUB * DAVID SWINSON *
AMOR TOWLES AND WILLY VLAUTIN

Illustrations by Ashley Newell Despain

Copyright © 2017 by
California Bookstore Day Publishing

Published exclusivley for
Independent Bookstore Day

First (and only) Edition

Printed in the United States of America
by Lightning Source, La Vergne, TN

Designed by Kristine Brogno
Illustrations by Ashley Newell Despain
Edited by Samantha Schoech

ISBN 978-0-9984499-1-3

All rights reserved.
No part of this book may be reproduced, scanned,
or distributed in any form without permission.

California Bookstore Day Publishing
A division of Independent Bookstore Day and
The Northern California Independent Booksellers Association
PO Box 280, Sonoma, CA 95476
www.indiebookstoreday.com

CONTENTS

THE HARD STUFF * 7

tequila, mezcal, vodka, gin, scotch, bourbon, rye, whiskey, picon

---

WINE & BUBBLES * 53

just like it sounds

MOCKTAILS * 67

virgin recipes

— Origin Ingredients —

CORN   GRAPES   WHEAT

SUGAR CANE    PEAT   POTATO

SUGAR BEET   MONKEY PUZZLE TREE   RYE

 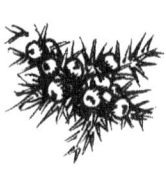 

RICE   JUNIPER BERRY   BLUE AGAVE

JAMES PATTERSON
LINDSAY BOXER'S MARGARITA

Few things in life are better than enjoying drinks with great friends. For one of my most popular characters, Detective Lindsay Boxer, a night of margaritas with buddies led to the creation of the Women's Murder Club, an unstoppable crime-solving team. Over the years—and what will soon be sixteen novels—these four friends always make time for margaritas and Mexican food at their favorite bar, Susie's.

Hopefully my writing of these scenes imparts a heady enough experience to take the edge off your day. But, if you're among friends—and don't feel like reading aloud to them—I thought you might appreciate Susie's recipe. It's the perfect drink for a fun night of catching up with friends and discussing your latest murder investigation. Cheers!

1.5 oz tequila

1 oz Cointreau (orange liqueur)

0.75 oz freshly squeezed lime juice

Ice

Optional: simple syrup for sweetening

Optional: lime wedge and salt for rimming the glass

If you would like a salt-rimmed glass, run a lime slice around the top rim of a glass. Dip the rim in a plate of salt until it is covered. Set it aside.

Add the tequila, lime juice, and Cointreau to a cocktail shaker, and shake or stir until combined. Taste, and if you would like it to be sweeter, stir in a splash of simple syrup.

Fill glass with ice. Pour in the margarita mixture. Garnish with an extra lime wedge.

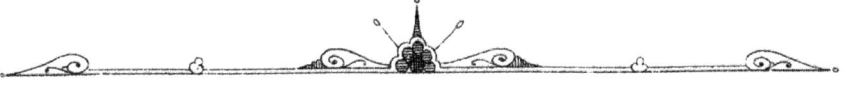

BETH LISICK
PALOMA

Oh, how I love to drink. I love to drink so much that I often tell myself: Remember to drink less so that in the future you are still able to drink more. I am partial to classic cocktails - martinis in the summer and manhattans in the winter - though if you run into me at a bar and I am out for the long haul, I could be on a tear with tequila and sodas. If you love tequila, it means you probably never got wasted on it when you were a teenager, and it also means you just might enjoy mezcal. Also made from agave, it's smoky and intense and, in my opinion, not an "everyday drinker." I think of it as Special Occasion booze.

I came across this mezcal cocktail on a snowy December night about a year and a half after moving to New York from Berkeley. I was still excited to be in a new place, but I was also feeling deflated about not having any friends to hang out with. (If you know how to "make friends" with a new person after the age of 45, get at me.) So we get invited to a party by someone my husband Eli was working with. He's a recording engineer and sometimes works with people I'm a total fan of. The party was a big deal because 1) I had been to exactly one other party the whole time I'd been in New York and 2) it was at the home of Yuka Honda (of the great band Cibo Matto), guitarist Nels Cline, and Sean Lennon. They all lived together in a brownstone in the Village like some kind of rock and roll fairytale. Hey, if I wasn't going to have friends, at least I could get drunk in the presence of the extraordinarily talented! Yuka was making these cocktails all night. She was eyeballing it, but it's a version of the Mexican Paloma that I've made many times since.

2 oz mezcal

2 oz freshly squeezed grapefruit juice. (Don't bother if you're not going to squeeze it yourself.)

3 oz club soda

Fill a glass with ice. Mezcal first, then grapefruit juice, then the soda. Garnish it with a grapefruit slice! Put fancy salt on the rim if you want! Hit me up if you're in New York and want to hang out!

MEZCAL

EDAN LEPUCKI
THE SOPHIA LORENZO

FAVORITE COCKTAIL: I have many favorite cocktails. I love French 75s, margaritas, sidecars, Manhattans, Pisco sours, and more. If it's fancy and cold, perhaps with a ribbon of lemon peel floating in its depths, serve it to me, please.

Lately, my favorite cocktail is a Negroni made with mezcal instead of gin. It's an Italian drink by way of Mexico. Let's call it...The Sophia Lorenzo.

The Sophia Lorenzo is made with Campari, sweet vermouth, and mezcal and like a Negroni it's refreshing and slightly medicinal-tasting. Ideal for summer. The mezcal, though, makes it taste smoky. There's a richness to it that I love. Be careful, though: Sophia Lorenzo is beautiful—but dangerous. Only drink one—or else.

FIRST TIME: I tried this cocktail (by a name I can't recall) at Pizzaiolo, a restaurant in Oakland whose drinks are only matched by their amazing wood-fired pizza. That night my family and I sat on their back patio, near their garden, under a lovely blue summer sky. A movie star was eating a few feet away from us, and as I sipped my drink, I stared at him, as if invisible. (I mean, I was invisible—he definitely wasn't looking at me.)

I made my own version the next weekend, and it was just as tasty as the restaurant's.

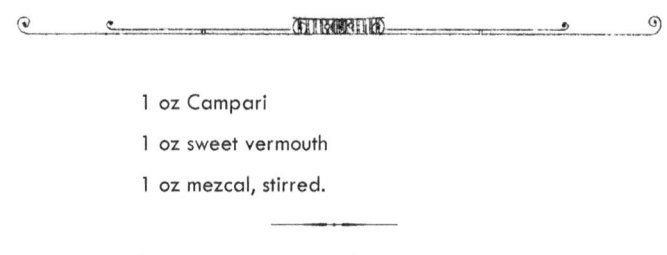

1 oz Campari

1 oz sweet vermouth

1 oz mezcal, stirred.

Pour over ice in a tumbler, or serve it "up" in a chilled Martini glass.

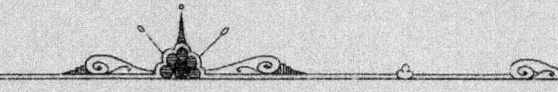

JULIA GLASS
JULIA'S GLASS

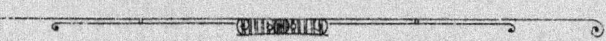

As I hardly need explicate, this potion was formulated expressly for me—an honor arguably commensurate with any of the major book awards—on April 12, 2016, at Bo's Kitchen & Bar in Manhattan. It was concocted for a book event I shared with the poet Ruth Danon and the short-story writer Kelly Fordon. When you've just turned sixty and have ruefully but responsibly relinquished a rent-stabilized apartment in the West Village to settle in a Brigadoonish town way up in New England, what's not to love about an invitation to return to your beloved New York and costar at a reading series called #YeahYouWrite, held in a subterranean lounge where the menu features fried alligator, the bartender will design a cocktail based on your favorite spirits, and you'll get to regale the audience (okay, mostly your old friends who did not defect from the city) with that story about the worst review you ever received, for your first novel, in *People* magazine, a review that led your take-no-prisoners publicist to shout at you over the phone, "Now you know how Julia Roberts feels!" while you stood in your parents' kitchen, pajama-clad and tearful, feeling like you were twelve all over again? Twitter-averse though I may be, I got a kick out of fraternizing with a hashtag, and best of all, I now have a recipe for a killer cocktail that just might carry my name into posterity as reliably as one of my books. Take that, *People*.

2 mint leaves, torn

1.5 oz tequila

0.5 oz pear liqueur

1 oz lime juice

0.5 oz agave syrup

Prosecco

Place torn mint in a cocktail shaker.

Add tequila, pear liqueur, lime juice, and syrup.

Shake with ice.

Strain into a chilled flute and top with prosecco.

BEST COCKTAIL CHATTER TOPIC: Anything but the recent election and what it portends.

FOOLPROOF HANGOVER CURE: In a perfect world, this formula works wonders for me (and probably only me):

Milky coffee + the love of two shaggy dogs + a New York Times acrostic puzzle + my older son at the piano (and a long, lazy morning in which to enjoy it all, younger son and his dad QUIETLY reading the paper)

AMOR TOWLES
THE LONG GOODBYE

"I like bars just after they open for the evening. When the air inside is still cool and clean and everything is shiny and the barkeep is giving himself that last look in the mirror to see if his tie is straight and his hair is smooth. I like the neat bottles on the bar back and the lovely shining glasses and the anticipation. I like to watch the man mix the first one of the evening and put it down on a crisp mat and put the little folded napkin beside it. I like to taste it slowly. The first quiet drink of the evening in a quiet bar—that's wonderful."

So says the hard-drinking Terry Lennox to Raymond Chandler's hard-boiled detective, Philip Marlowe, as they sit in Victor's in Los Angeles circa 1950 in the opening chapters of *The Long Goodbye*. In the novel, Marlowe befriends Lennox by joining him regularly at a bar for a few rounds of Lennox's favorite drink: a gimlet. Having launched their ill-fated friendship, this luminescent cocktail becomes a motif in the novel. The drink comes to represent Marlowe's fondness for Lennox—a sentimental order that the detective places when Lennox disappears in the aftermath of his wife's murder. The drink serves as a clue when Marlowe observes a mysterious woman ordering one at Victor's, suggesting she too must have ties to Lennox. And ultimately, the drink punctuates the end of a friendship when Marlowe refuses to have one in the novel's closing pages.

Every summer, I treat myself to reading the novels of a great crime writer in chronological order. Having worked through an array of authors over the years, I have taken particular pleasure in reading the works of Dashiell Hammett, Raymond Chandler, and Ross McDonald—each of whom are collected in multi-volume sets by the Library of America (the non-profit publisher of America's greatest writing). In reading the seven novels included in the LOA's two Chandler editions, you get to enjoy not simply the oeuvre of one of America's greatest crime writers, you get to immerse yourself in the seedy glamor of Los Angeles as it evolves from the late 1930s to the late 1950s.

As an added bonus, you can complement your reading of Chandler's work by watching the movies based on his books—which include some of the greatest examples of American film noir: Howard Hawks's *The Big Sleep* (1946) with Humphrey Bogart as Marlowe; *Murder, My Sweet* (1944) with Dick Powell in the role; and *The Lady in the Lake* (1947) with Robert Montgomery. Then you can cap off this 1940s film fest with Roger Altman's divinely weird interpretation of *The Long Goodbye* (1973) set in 1970s L.A. with Elliot Gould as a hipster version of Chandler's detective.

Anyway, when I was reading the works of Chandler a few summers ago and I finally got to *The Long Goodbye*, I would eagerly wait for dusk so I could make myself a gimlet, pick up the book, and join Marlowe in some gloomy corner of Los Angeles.

In *The Long Goodbye,* Lennox insists that a gimlet should be made with gin and Rose's lime juice.

I agree with Lennox that a gimlet should be made with gin, but I insist upon making mine with freshly-squeezed juice. The fresh lime juice gives the cocktail a welcome tartness, and with the appropriate overhead lighting it also ensures a perfectly luminescent drink. A lime and gin cocktail has gone by the name gimlet since the 1920s, but under the right conditions it could just as easily be called The Long Goodbye.

2 oz gin

1 oz freshly squeezed lime juice

1 teaspoon super fine sugar (or simple syrup)

Shaken with ice, served up in the smallest martini glass you can find. Best appreciated when drunk in the company of a charismatic boozer who has a fancy house and a shady past.

KAREN ABBOTT
GIN RICKEY

My next book (tentatively titled *A Vast and Vulgar Beauty: Murder, Revenge, and Justice in the Jazz Age*) tells the true story of bootlegger George Remus. In the early Twenties, in the span of two years, he amassed a fortune of $25 million dollars. He threw lavish parties in his Cincinnati mansion, giving away cars and watches and diamond stick pins, and slipping money under his guests' dinner plates. As the story goes, F. Scott Fitzgerald reportedly met Remus at a Kentucky hotel, and was so taken with the bootlegger's savvy and charisma that he was inspired to create Jay Gatsby. Ironically, Remus was a lifelong teetotaler, so here's a recipe for one of Gatsby's favorite cocktails, the Gin Rickey.

Put three or four ice cubes in a highball glass, and squeeze in the juice of half a lime. Add around 2 ounces of gin, and top with soda. Rub the lime wedge around the rim, then drop into the glass.

And that's it! Simple, refreshing, potent.

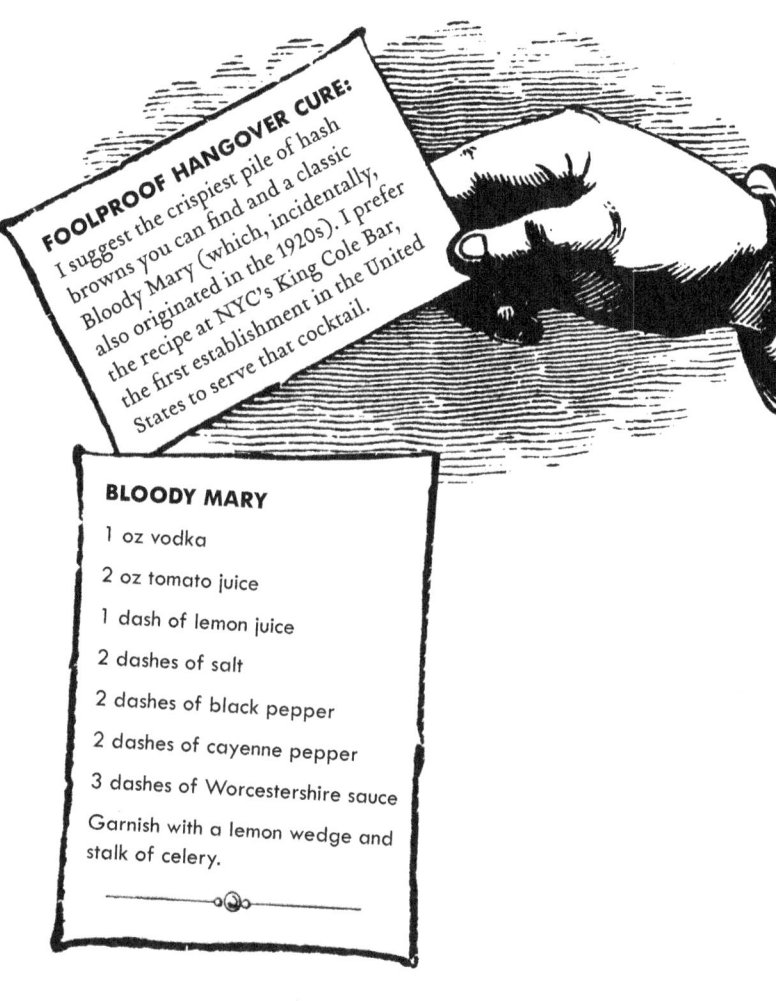

FOOLPROOF HANGOVER CURE:
I suggest the crispiest pile of hash browns you can find and a classic Bloody Mary (which, incidentally, also originated in the 1920s). I prefer the recipe at NYC's King Cole Bar, the first establishment in the United States to serve that cocktail.

BLOODY MARY

1 oz vodka

2 oz tomato juice

1 dash of lemon juice

2 dashes of salt

2 dashes of black pepper

2 dashes of cayenne pepper

3 dashes of Worcestershire sauce

Garnish with a lemon wedge and stalk of celery.

AMY STEWART
MAMANI GIN & TONIC

It's astonishing to look back, from the comforts of the twenty-first century, at the hardships that early plant explorers endured. In 1865, a British sheep trader living in Peru thought he had tracked down a species of cinchona tree whose bark had the highest levels of quinine, a chemical used as a malaria treatment. This was no small matter, as previous attempts to cultivate cinchona trees and harvest the bark for malaria medicine had failed. Plant explorers kept bringing back other varieties that just didn't produce enough quinine.

But this sheep trader somehow got hold of the right seeds. He just couldn't figure out how to get them out of Peru. The Peruvian people were not exactly happy with Europeans plundering their jungles in search of medicine, which made seed-smuggling a dangerous operation.

The only solution was to foist the job off on a manservant. Manuel Incra Mamani was the native Peruvian unlucky enough to be assigned this task. On his journey across the country he was robbed, imprisoned, beaten, starved, and eventually died—but he did smuggle those seeds out of Peru.

That's how quinine—a malaria medicine and the bitter ingredient in tonic water—made it to the British Empire. I named this drink after him, because the Manuel Incra Mamanis of the world never get enough credit.

This is a variation on many fancy gin and tonics I've had over the years. I like a cocktail that's not too sweet, not too fruity, and not too acidic, which leaves out most of them. This, on the other hand, is a savory, spicy, vegetal drink that tastes more like a salad in a glass. I'm pretty sure it counts as a daily vegetable serving.

Oh, and whatever you do, don't drink that cheap, mass-market tonic water, or Manuel Incra Mamani will have died in vain. Get a high-quality tonic like Fever Tree instead, or mix club soda with one of the many fine tonic syrups now on the market.

1.5 oz gin

2-3 fresh jalapeño slices (or, if you prefer, a milder pepper), seeds removed

2-3 sprigs cilantro or basil

2-3 chunks cucumber

1 chunk celery stalk

4 oz high-quality tonic water

1-2 cherry tomatoes, along with a basil or cilantro leaf, on a pick for garnish

Ice

Fill a Mason jar, Collins glass, or short tumbler with ice. In between the ice cubes, layer in a few slices of cucumber, pepper, a sprig of cilantro or basil, and a cherry tomato.

In a cocktail shaker, combine the first five ingredients. Use a muddler or wooden spoon to gently crush the vegetables and herbs. Then add ice and shake well.

Strain the gin and pour over ice. Fill the glass with tonic water. Garnish with a cherry tomato and basil or cilantro leaf on a pick.

SLOANE CROSLEY
FRENCH 75

FAVORITE COCKTAIL: For starters, it's the only cocktail I can make. I mean, I can make a martini. I can make a vodka and soda. I am, after all, a person. But a French 75 is involved. It takes effort and it's unusual but sophisticated. Some people make it with vodka instead of gin. Or cognac. Those people are lunatics.

FIRST TIME: I discovered it right after I graduated from college. In college everything came out of a bottle or a red Solo cup. I was reading an old—like vintage old—issue of *Esquire* and I thought it would be fun to make. Plus, I had recently been gifted a cocktail shaker. So I got pretty good at making them and my own version became my favorite. That has never happened with any other drink or food I've made.

The Fitzgerald way:

One large Frenchman

One gallon gin

75 oz bitters

Snake

The real way:

Juice of 1 lemon

1.5 oz gin (the good stuff)

2 oz Champagne or sparkling wine (the pretty good stuff)

1 Tbsp simple syrup

Shake everything with ice.

Pour into a chilled champagne glass. Garnish with lemon peel. Drink should be ice cold.

MOLLY PRENTISS
NEGRONI

FAVORITE COCKTAIL: A classic Negroni, because it's bitter and sweet and strong, and it makes you feel cozy in winter and cool in summer.

FIRST TIME: I first had a Negroni when living in Italy when I was a sophomore in college. At the time, I didn't like its bitter flavor, and could barely drink it. But years later I had it again, at a bar in Brooklyn, and afterward I couldn't stop craving the bitter taste of the Campari. Now it's my go-to drink. In deep summer, I sometimes order the Negroni's cousin, a Campari Spritz (white wine, Campari, soda water, slice of orange), as a lighter, fresh alternative.

1 part dry gin

1 part Campari

1 part sweet Italian vermouth

Orange peel

Shake well with ice. Strain into chilled glass (Old Fashioned glass works well) over ice (preferably one large ice cube, so it melts slowly and evenly). Garnish with twisty orange peel.

BEST COCKTAIL CHATTER: Books, of course! (This quickly devolves after the first cocktail.)

FOOLPROOF HANGOVER CURE: The European equivalent of Asprin, called Asprina C. You put a tablet in water and it fizzes like Alka Seltzer. Cures a headache and forces you to drink water at the same time. I'm also big on hair of the dog—drink a single beer at around 2pm the day after for optimal results.

HOMER HICKAM
SKYRIDGE BREEZE

My favorite cocktail is a drink called Skyridge Breeze. It was invented at our home we call Skyridge in St. John, U.S. Virgin Islands. It was an instant hit.

When we heard a hurricane was bearing down on us in the fall of 2014, my buddy Al English, who was our guest at the time, and I experimented with the contents of my pantry and the local rum and created this delicious, refreshing drink.

Skyridge Breeze is the perfect cocktail to boost morale when all else fails. Examples of moments such as these would be when your publisher fails to pick up your book proposal, or your movie options go out of date with no action by the producers, or your IRS bill is a lot more than you thought it was going to be, or your wife is unhappy over something you did that you didn't think was so bad at the time, or when your cats rip your sofa to shreds.

If this or anything like this is your situation, you need a Skyridge Breeze. Here's the recipe:

1. Find a tumbler.
2. Put ice in the tumbler.
3. Add to tumbler:

   1 shot gin

   1 shot (or two) dark rum (unspiced)

   3 oz Crystal Lite Lemon powder drink

   1 tsp of lime juice

   Top off with Ginger Beer

4. Mix irresolutely as befits your mental turmoil.
5. If possible, sit down and look at the Caribbean (a photo will do).
6. Contemplate the beauty. Listen to the birds. If there are no birds, whistle softly to yourself.
7. Drink slowly.
8. Repeat if necessary (it's almost always necessary).
9. Allow a sigh and go on with life.

KATE SCHATZ
ALAMEDA G&T + THE CURE

FAVORITE COCKTAIL: I'd like to offer two cocktails for California's two distinct seasons:

Summerish: The Alameda G+T, because a gin and tonic is the perfect summerish cocktail. I say "summerish" because much of the year is like summer in California. Once it gets sunny and warm and I can wear flip-flops without my feet getting too cold, it is time for G+Ts. This particular one is, as we in the Bay Area like to say, hyperlocal. Made with St. George Terroir gin and limes from my backyard, it is best enjoyed in my backyard.

Winterish: The Cure, because it is what I drink when it gets "cold" here, and it is especially great when I have a cold. It's a classic hot toddy situation, with the addition of cayenne pepper and grated ginger. It's soothing, warming, and obviously very healthy and healing.

FIRST TIME: I've always loved a good G+T. When we moved to Alameda we realized that we were in biking distance from the wonderful St. George distillery. We sampled their goods and, while I love pretty much everything they make, the Terroir gin is my fave. It's made from botanicals harvested on Mt. Tamalpais (which, while not in Alameda, is visible from some parts of the city).

As for The Cure: My mom loves to make a hot toddy, and I like to make really intense fire water potions when I'm sick. I combined the two for a healing cocktail vibe.

Let it be known that I am a terribly inexact person, so all "recipes" are vague estimates.

Alameda G+T

Pour a good glug of St. George Terroir gin over a few rocks. I find a good highball glass to be ideal—a few times I've ordered G+Ts and had them come in pint glasses, which I think is really gross for some reason.

Anyway: pour gin over ice, add a splash of good tonic (Fever Tree or Q or, if you're very fancy, something "housemade").

Then go into my backyard (with my permission, ok?) and get some limes and squeeze at least one.

Mix, then drink it with me in the backyard. Pet my dog, bring your kids.

Bonus points if you bring over some chips + guac.

The Cure

Boil some water.

Locate a favorite mug.

Pour a big glug of blue-state whiskey (post-election, my husband is committed to blue state whiskey only).

Add a good squeeze of honey, the juice of several fresh lemons, a decent amount of grated ginger, and a dash or two of cayenne.

Fill the rest of the mug with hot hot water, and stir.

Sit on the couch and sip while blowing your nose and watching something decent on TV.

Bonus points if a cat curls up on your lap.

BEST COCKTAIL CHATTER: The story of why I always have a paper napkin wadded up in my right hand at cocktail parties. Ask me about it next time you see me.

FOOLPROOF HANGOVER CURE: Have children who wake up really, really early. That's an excellent reason for me to not have that "one last drink."

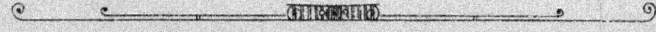

— Tools of the Trade —

SHAKER　　STRAINER　　JIGGER　　POUR SPOUT

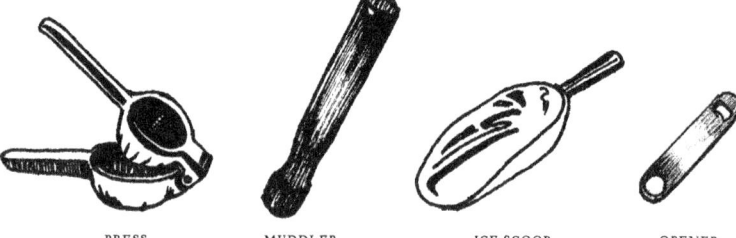

PRESS　　MUDDLER　　ICE SCOOP　　OPENER

WINE KEY　　STIR SPOON　　SILLY STRAW　　ZESTER

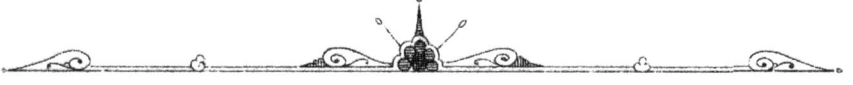

LAUREN GROFF
VODKA MARTINI

FAVORITE COCKTAIL: I love a Tito's vodka martini, vermouth wafted swiftly over the surface of the drink, with many extra olives. On Fridays, after my little boys have their piano lessons, we all go out together to a restaurant called The Top a few blocks from our house in Gainesville, Florida. I order one of these, and as soon as I have it in my hand, my whole body relaxes into the weekend. It's a pure cold burst of relief.

FIRST TIME: I used to drink only beer—I was an intern at Brewery Ommegang in Cooperstown one summer—then only wine, after I spent a year in France, and then only bourbon after a fellowship year in Louisville, when Pappy VanWinkles was easy to find and cheap-ish. But with kids, I needed something stronger, especially if I was saving up my drinks for Friday nights. I ordered my first vodka martini at The Top shortly after my first son was born, out of post-partum despair, and never looked back. We walk home.

Tito's vodka

a very cold martini glass, with a few drops of vermouth sprinkled in, then shaken out

6 big olives

Put vodka into a martini shaker with ice, shake for far longer than seems reasonable, pour into the glass, put olives in, drink half immediately, feel better about writing and life as you listen to your children fight in the opposite booth.

MIN JIN LEE
MIDORI MELON BALL

Fall 1986, New Haven, Connecticut
Cocktails at Durfee Hall—hosted by Sarah, Germaine, and me.
The Melon Ball is a swirly green color, and it smells like Japanese melon candy.

In 1986, when I was eighteen years old, some friends and I threw a cocktail party in our freshman dorm. Our pal Tony made up letterpress-printed invitations for the event, and we sent them to a hundred freshmen. We decided to serve Melon Balls and Fuzzy Navels, because the drink names sounded sexy. At the party, we wore red lipstick and glittering thrift shop dresses while fending off the overflow of sweaty bodies clamoring for syrupy drinks. It was the height of juvenile pretension, but for a few sequined moments, we thought we were quite glamorous.

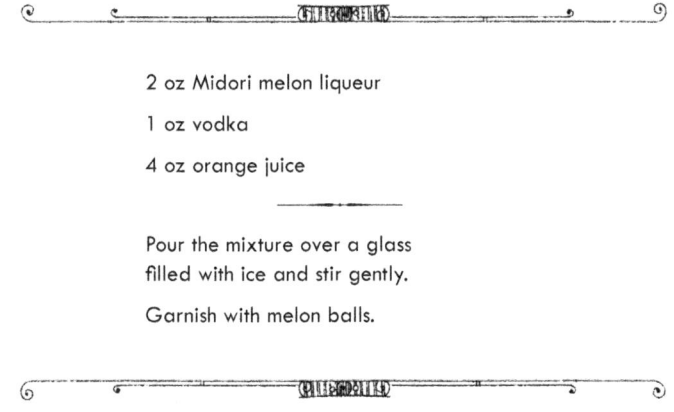

2 oz Midori melon liqueur

1 oz vodka

4 oz orange juice

Pour the mixture over a glass filled with ice and stir gently.

Garnish with melon balls.

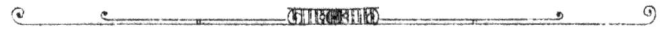

BEST COCKTAIL CHATTER: In the Northeast corridor and especially in New York City, cocktail party guests lean heavily on real estate, holiday spots, or schools for chatter topics. Interestingly, when strangers find out that I write fiction, they open up a bit. Men tell me about affairs and women about divorces. I can talk moderately well about finance and even better about lost loves.

FOOLPROOF HANGOVER CURE: Nope. I've never had a hangover because after one drink, I turn red and feel sleepy.

LOUIS BAYARD
VODKA TONIC

FAVORITE COCKTAIL: I am embarrassed to admit how proletarian my favorite cocktail is, but it's your basic vodka tonic. Nominally a summer drink but it works for me in all weathers, and if I'm the one mixing, it never disappoints.

FIRST TIME: In the bygone days of college, I was the vice president of a musical-theater group. Every month or so, we would have to meet with the alumni board of trustees to defend whatever rash or ill-considered decisions we had made with money that was not ours. I found the experience stressful enough that I began to look for something a little harder than beer. As it turned out, the suavest and handsomest and best-smelling of the trustees was drinking a vodka tonic, so I ordered the same, and it was love at first drink.

Oh, this isn't too hard. You pour in a healthy amount of vodka, and then you add what I would call a chaser of tonic water. Most every bar in the land will attempt to reverse that formula, so if you don't want vodka-flavored sugar water, you might consider asking for a double vodka with "a splash" of tonic. (And how that word "splash" makes me think of George H. W. Bush, for whom I've grown inordinately wistful.) If you want to put on airs, you may throw in a wedge of lime or lemon, but it's not necessary. The vodka will carry all before it, so don't economize with Gilbey's. But don't feel you need to go all Grey Goose, either.

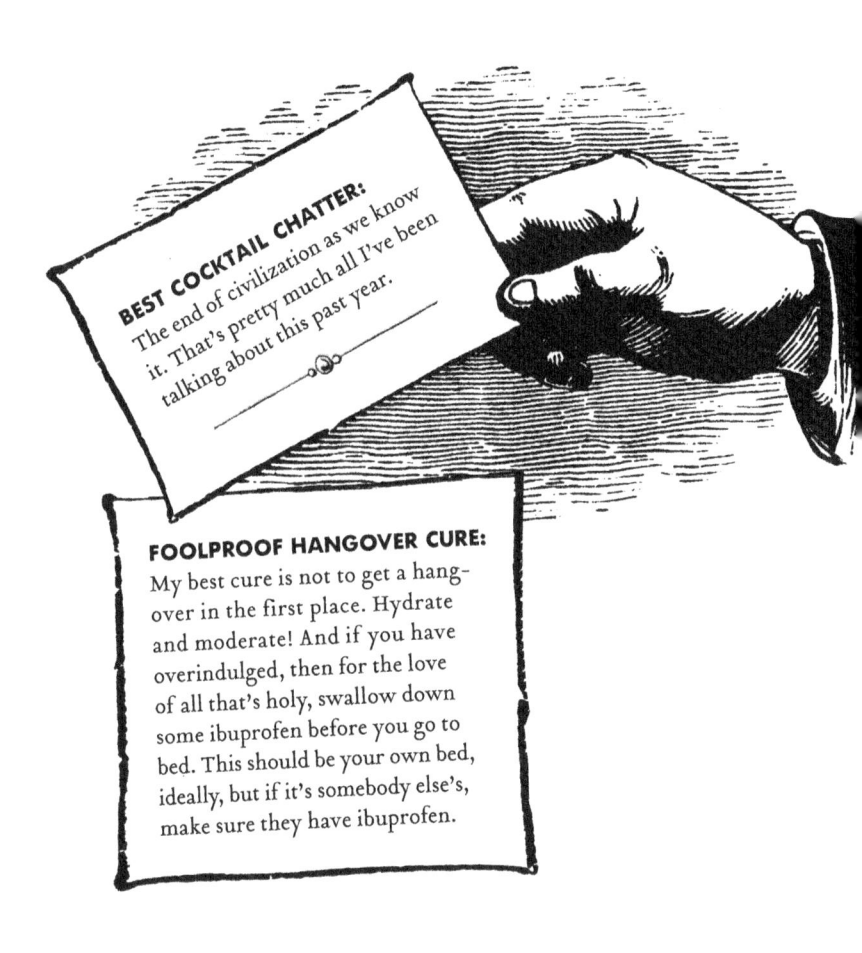

BEST COCKTAIL CHATTER:
The end of civilization as we know it. That's pretty much all I've been talking about this past year.

FOOLPROOF HANGOVER CURE:
My best cure is not to get a hangover in the first place. Hydrate and moderate! And if you have overindulged, then for the love of all that's holy, swallow down some ibuprofen before you go to bed. This should be your own bed, ideally, but if it's somebody else's, make sure they have ibuprofen.

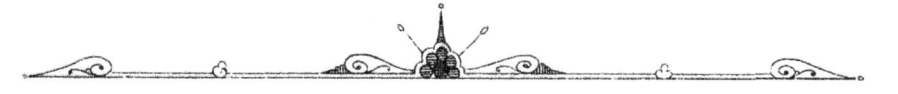

JACQUELINE LUCKETT
DIRTY MARTINI

FAVORITE COCKTAIL: I'm a wine lover at heart, but on those occasions when I do have a cocktail, it's a dirty martini. But it took a while to acquire a taste for that strong drink.

FIRST TIME: In my 20s, I fell in love with New York and what I believed to be all things representative of that amazing, sophisticated city. So, it seemed quite natural to choose what I believed to be the ultimate in sophisticated cocktails—a martini.

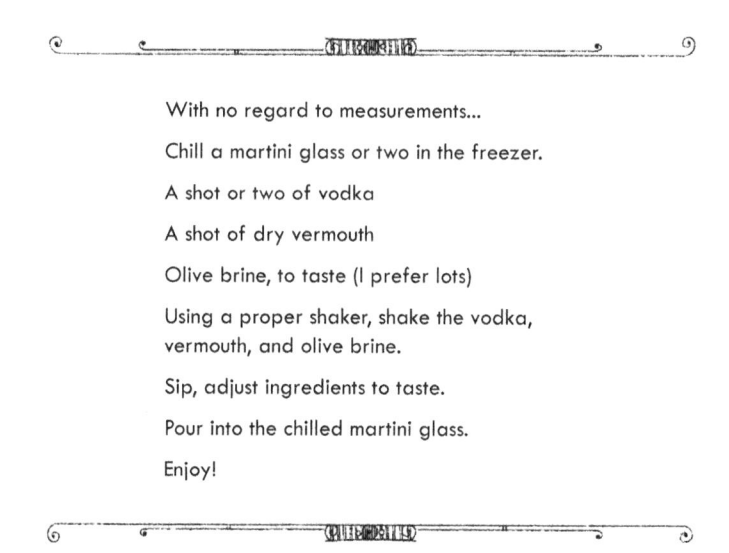

With no regard to measurements...

Chill a martini glass or two in the freezer.

A shot or two of vodka

A shot of dry vermouth

Olive brine, to taste (I prefer lots)

Using a proper shaker, shake the vodka, vermouth, and olive brine.

Sip, adjust ingredients to taste.

Pour into the chilled martini glass.

Enjoy!

BEST COCKTAIL CHATTER: With so many issues to discuss these days, my choice is sticking to light conversation. Paris is my favorite topic for starters—have you been, when are you going, have you read my books? They're an armchair visit to the City of Light.

FOOLPROOF HANGOVER CURE: I pride myself on not having hangovers these days. My solution isn't a cure, but it sure helps. For every cocktail, I drink a full glass of cool water. And if all else fails, I make sure to take two ibuprofen tablets before going to bed. Works every time.

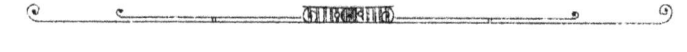

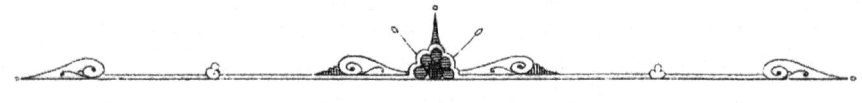

VIET THANH NGUYEN
THE SYMPATHIZER

FAVORITE COCKTAIL: Trying to pick my favorite cocktail is like trying to pick a favorite child. I love them all.

My favorite drink is actually not a cocktail, but Scotch. The older the better. Unlike cocktails, Scotch is always reliable and not dependent on the talents of your bartender or mixologist. This is important when you, the writer, are alone at night after a long day of writing and want a quick solution to the problems of the world (or just your writing). My current favorite is Glenfiddich 18. Neat.

FIRST TIME: My first Scotch was in Saigon, 2004, where one could buy bottles of Balvenie Doublewood for a very low price of about $33. I've never seen it again for such a bargain and had at least one bottle a week for the several months that I lived in Saigon. This was the beginning of my predilection for Scotch. As for Glenfiddich 18, it is a recent discovery.

If I have to give you a recipe for a cocktail, then of course I will provide you with the one for The Sympathizer, as concocted by Andrea Tetrick, book representative extraordinaire and a very early supporter of the novel. She served this at the book launch for the novel.

The Sympathizer mixture:

equal parts

Bourbon

Aperol

Cynar

Lemon juice

1 oz of the Sympathizer mixture and wait to top off with 2 oz of Champagne or sparkling wine

BOURBON/RYE/WHISKEY

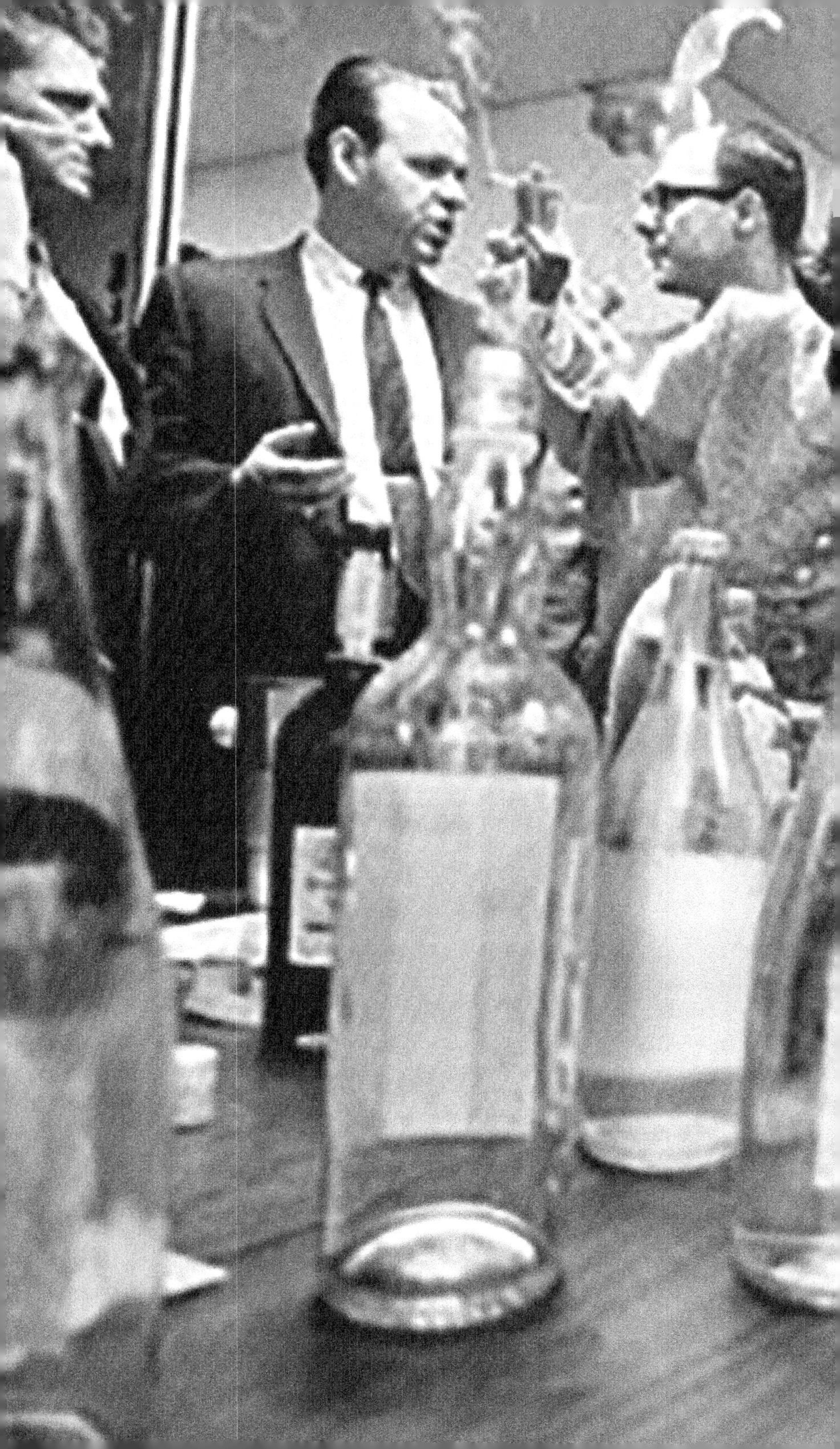

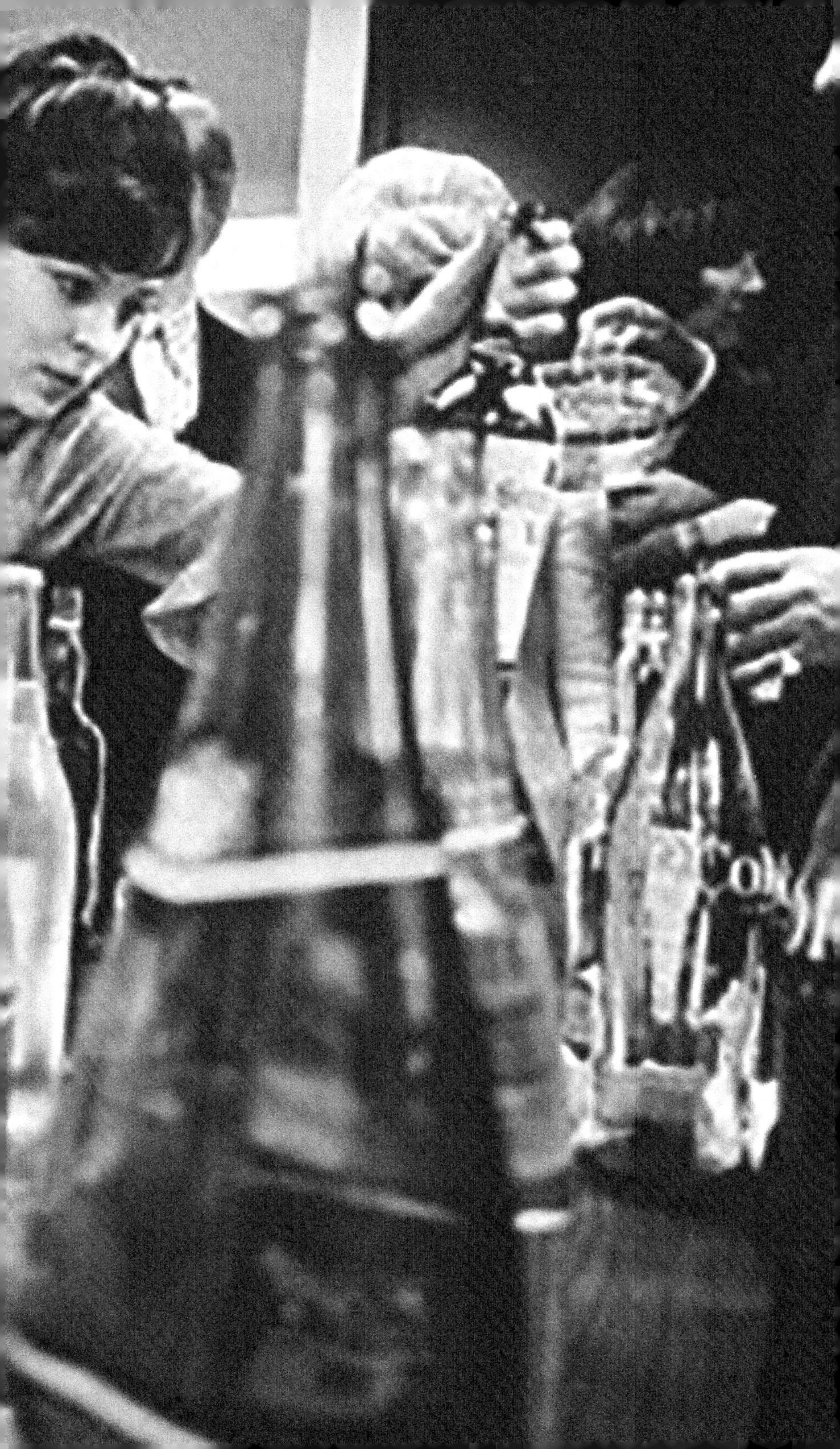

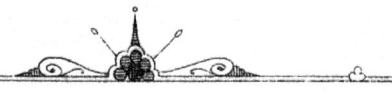

JOSHILYN JACKSON
THE BOSS LADY

FAVORITE COCKTAIL: The Boss Lady, because it was invented especially for me, and it stars all the liquors I like best.

FIRST TIME: My husband invented it; He calls me Boss Lady sometimes, and I discovered Boss Lady bitters during a trip to Asheville, North Carolina. Scott said it was a sign that he needed to invent a signature drink for me. There was a lot of delicious trial and error before he hit on the exact right thing. This is a big, boozy drink for people who enjoy the taste of liquor.

1.5 oz Buffalo Trace bourbon

0.75 oz Bénédictine

0.75 oz Luxardo

1 barspoon vermouth

1 healthy dropper of Boss Lady Floral Bitters

1 Drunken Cherry (This is a jarred maraschino cherry preserved in liquor. Woodford Reserve makes a nice bourbon version, or Williams-Sonoma has them in Luxardo. If you like a sweeter drink, use a regular maraschino and add a splash of juice from the jar.)

Serve room temperature in a large snifter, or shake over ice and serve up in a Champagne coupe.

BEST COCKTAIL CHATTER: Books, of course! Though mixology is a close second. I was a bartender in a former life, and I still love coming up with new ways to tipple. My favorite was invented in tandem with narrative non-fiction writer Karen Abbott at the now sadly defunct Fairhope Writer's Conference down in Alabama. It has an unprintable name: The ****tini. If you want help filling in the asterisks, I will tell you it featured a garnish made of two maraschino cherries and a length of red Twizzler arranged as pornographically as possible upon a toothpick. The toothpick was then placed crosswise on the cup's edge, so that the cherry-framed Twizzler dangled down into the glass. I can't remember the exact recipe, but it contained gin, white cranberry juice, and something else that made it bright blue. It swilled with great abandon by a host of writers including Tom Franklin, Beth Ann Fennelly, and Sonny Brewer.

FOOLPROOF HANGOVER CURE: Yes—never have more than two Boss Ladies! It is a pre-emptive cure. But should that fail, a huge bowl of cheese grits with crumbled bacon and a ton of butter will soak up last night's poison.

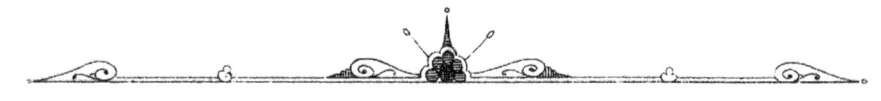

DANIEL HANDLER
OLD-FASHIONED

FAVORITE COCKTAIL: The Old-Fashioned, because, like life, it often involves a bit of improvisation, and, even when it doesn't taste good, it tastes good enough.

FIRST TIME: I was introduced to this cocktail the first time I met my literary agent. Chronology tells me that I was in my mid-twenties but I felt five years old. I had agreed to meet her for a drink at her hotel bar, and the whole thing - an agent, meeting for drinks, a hotel bar - was glamorous and foreign to me. She ordered an Old-Fashioned, and, me too, because what did I know?

The Old-Fashioned consists of three parts: the muddle, the kicker, and the fizz, just like life.

The muddle consists of some fruit and bitters one smashes up at the bottom of a glass. An orange slice and a maraschino cherry are standard, but you can use whatever fruity material you might find around: lemon peel, a few berries, a tablespoon of marmalade, gumdrops, chutney, fresh ginger, rosemary, and even applesauce are acceptable. Do not use a Now and Later—a mistake you only make once. Put the muddle in the bottom of a short, chubby glass and add some bitters, which requires no substitution, because no civilized household is without bitters. Some people like a sugar cube in there; personally I find it overkill and have heard that sugar is bad for you. Mash them with a pestle or a spoon or a nearby washable tchotchke.

The kicker is booze. Bourbon and rye are best. Other whiskies may be used in a pinch. Brandy works. Rum sort of works. Do not use gin. If you have nothing but gin, make it cold and call it a martini. Vodka is not being mentioned for a reason. Add two fingers of the kicker to the muddle and stir with ice.

The fizz is soda water. Ginger ale can be used in a pinch. Tonic can a little bit. Champagne can be used but you will soon find yourself engaged in notoriety. If you do not have these things, use nothing. Spritz a little fizz on the top of the glass and serve.

BEST COCKTAIL CHATTER: "Let's write some poems on these napkins."

FOOLPROOF HANGOVER CURE: A swim in cold water and a steamed barbeque pork bun, although I have also heard copious vomiting recommended.

*I like to utter a toast
I'm told is Palestinian:
"May we never suffer more than this."*

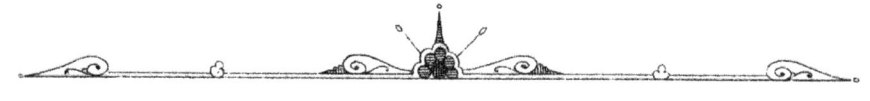

SAMUEL LIGON
THE LONELY MARTHA

Everybody knows George Washington cut down his father's cherry tree with a hatchet and couldn't lie about it. What most people don't know is that he also chopped off Thomas Jefferson's hands—with a gator knife—and then pretended he didn't. Jefferson was furious, of course. He took a glove between his teeth and threw it to the floor at Washington's feet. Everyone was really sad and surprised about Jefferson killing Washington with a dueling pistol when he didn't even have hands, but then Ben Franklin bucked America up by inventing electricity and a classic craft cocktail, slightly modified for our modern times below.

I first had The Lonely Martha the day after the 2016 election in the heartland of America right at the beginning of the end. Or maybe it was the middle of the end. Hard to tell.

A shrub

A hatchet

Whiskey

Sweet vermouth

Citrus

Two cherries

Bitters

Something to muddle

Dueling pistols

Find a shrub and chop it down with the hatchet. Admit that you've chopped it down. Open the case of dueling pistols. Close it. Make a Manhattan. I usually use bourbon, but you can also use rye. People in Wisconsin use brandy. No one knows why. The proportions are like this: 4 to 1 whiskey to vermouth. Or 10 to 1. Depending on how strong you want it. Some people will insist a Manhattan must be served up. That ice must not melt in it. Open the case of dueling pistols. These people should be shot. But, wait: you're making a cocktail. Muddle whatever it is you're going to muddle. Pour the whiskey and vermouth over ice or into a shaker. Stir it. Shake it. Stir it. I don't actually ever shake it. I stir it with my finger. Make yours however you want. Once the ice starts reacting with the whiskey, peel the citrus over the garbage can. Citrus doesn't belong in a Manhattan. Cherries do. Get the kind that don't look toxic. Dash in some bitters. Sip your drink. Admire the pistols. This is America. Sip again. Is the current president doing anything right? Who knows? Sip your drink and imagine how idiotic your face would look on money.

BEST COCKTAIL CHATTER: I like wide-ranging, nonsensical cocktail chatter, in languages I don't understand, about donkeys and goats.

FOOLPROOF HANGOVER CURE: Marching around the house to parade music for an hour is foolproof. As is a good old-fashioned tent revival, you and everyone around you sweating and quivering with joy and fear and the promise of salvation.

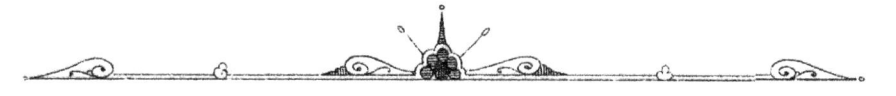

WILLY VLAUTIN
PICON PUNCH

I'm pretty low class. I'm 48 and just had my first martini this year. But the one cocktail I've been drinking since I was 15 or so is the Picon Punch. I grew up in Reno where there are two old school Basque restaurants. Northern Nevada had a great number of Basques who were sheepherders and when they were off the mountains they would come into town—Carson City, Reno, Winnemucca, and Elko—and stay at Basque hotel/rooming houses. The restaurants were an extension of that. The same meal served to everyone. Things now have changed but the Picon Punch hasn't. The American Basque cocktail. One is perfect, two you'll say weird things at dinner, and three will send you to your doom. They say, "Brother watch out, 'cause it's the drink that'll punch you back." It reminds me of Nevada and being a kid.

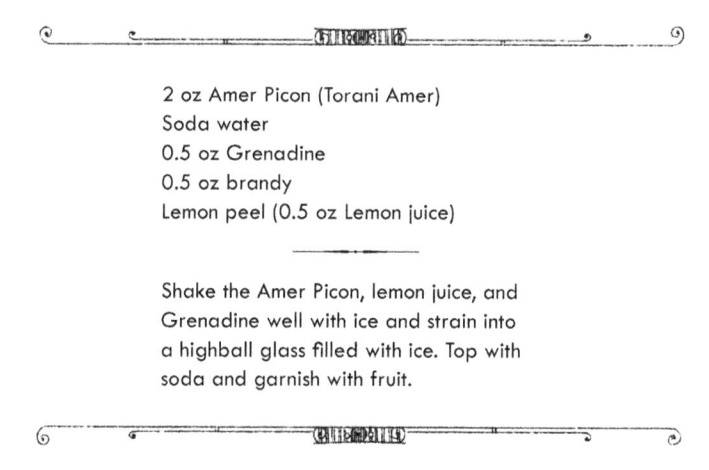

2 oz Amer Picon (Torani Amer)
Soda water
0.5 oz Grenadine
0.5 oz brandy
Lemon peel (0.5 oz Lemon juice)

Shake the Amer Picon, lemon juice, and Grenadine well with ice and strain into a highball glass filled with ice. Top with soda and garnish with fruit.

BEST COCKTAIL CHATTER: When I drink Picons I love to talk about Nevada and how I'm gonna buy a big ranch there some day. It's a line of day dreaming I've been having since I was in high school. The ranch and what's on it have now gotten more out of control and even more unrealistic except when I have a Picon in my hand. When I'm drinking those, the ranch is just outside the door.

FOOLPROOF HANGOVER CURE: I've tried them all. Sadly the only cure is not to drink. But you can't go wrong with tacos and "The Black Doctor" (Coke), a codeine tablet, and a day inside a movie theater.

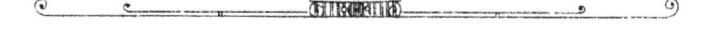

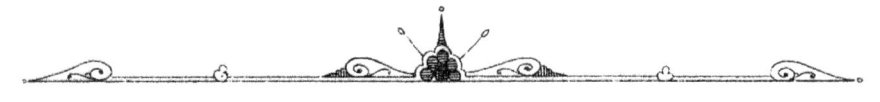

BRAD PARKS
THE ZOMBIE

FAVORITE COCKTAIL: The Zombie. I like it mostly for the story attached to its creation. Legend has it a businessman stumbled into Don the Beachcomber's in Hollywood, moaning he was hung over and saying he needed something to get him through a meeting. Don allegedly created this drink on the fly.

When the businessman came back later, Don asked if it had worked. The businessman replied that it had turned him into a zombie. Hence the drink's name.

Now, I believe that story about as much as I believe my novels are whipped up on the fly, with no editing, before being shipped to the printer. But who am I to deny someone their fiction?

FIRST TIME: I was at the summit of K2, which—as everyone knows—is also the finish line for the Himalayas Marathon. In my case, it was my second marathon in three days, but I don't want to talk about that, because I'll have to admit I did take a day off. But, hey, you gotta swim the English Channel sometime, you know?

Anyhow, there I was, at the finish line, when a Yeti came up out of nowhere. It turns out he spoke perfect English, albeit with a bit of an Australian accent, so I asked him to sit down for a drink. I just happened to have three different kinds of rum, bitters, Herbsaint, and some of the other ingredients listed below in my knapsack. The others I scrounged from the nearby flora.

In other words: There's no way I'm telling you that story.

0.75 oz fresh lime juice

0.5 oz Don's Mix[1]

0.5 oz falernum[2]

1.5 oz Gold Puerto Rican rum

1.5 oz aged Jamaican rum

1 oz 151-proof Lemon Hart Demerara rum[3]

1 dash Angostura bitters

6 drops Pernod or Herbsaint[4]

1 tsp Grenadine

6 oz crushed ice

Put it in a blender (or a Vitamix, because then you can say it's healthy). Blend at high speed for five seconds. Pour into a chimney glass. Add ice to fill. Garnish with a mint sprig.

[1] Two parts grapefruit juice, one part cinnamon syrup.

[2] You can make falernum at home. But, really, who has that kind of time?

[3] Or, instead of this exotic blend of rums, you can throw in four ounces of whatever swill you bought at the ABC Store and call it a day.

[4] This is an absinthe substitute, so it probably won't make you cut your ear off. If only Van Gogh had known.

NOTE: I stole this recipe, minus the footnotes, from *Professor Cocktail's Zombie Horde: Recipes for the World's Most Lethal Drink* by David J. Montgomery, a.k.a. Professor Cocktail. He, in turn, seems to have stolen it from *Beachbum Berry's Sippin' Safari* by Jeff Berry.

BEST COCKTAIL CHATTER: I find "What have you read lately?" to be a fine conversation starter.

FOOLPROOF HANGOVER CURE: With all apologies to Elizabeth Kübler-Ross, I believe in the Stages of Hangover Recovery. Much like Kübler-Ross's Stages of Grief, Stage One is denial. But that never works, so that's where my model diverges. Stage Two is Extra Strength Tylenol. Stage Three is Gatorade, preferably orange, but any color will do. Stage Four is napping. Stage Five is bacon—club sandwich, bacon cheeseburger, or just straight bacon (chased by pancakes, naturally). I repeat Stages Four and Five as many times as needed until the throbbing goes away.

Barware

WATER GOBLET	 RED WINE	 WHITE WINE	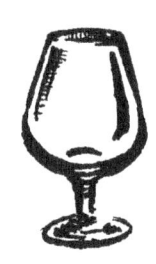 BRANDY
 MARTINI	 TRADITIONAL CHAMPAGNE		 CHAMPAGNE FLUTE
 ZOMBIE	 OLD FASHIONED	 SHOT GLASS	 PORT
 COCKTAIL MONKEY + UMBRELLA		 TIKI MUG	 MASON JAR

WINE & BUBBLES

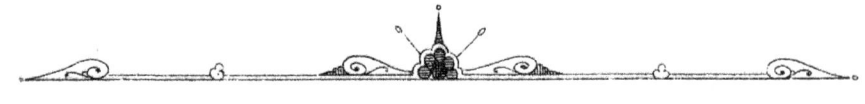

EMMA STRAUB
THE CHAMPAGNE NECESSITY

My favorite cocktail is a cool, bubbly glass of champagne. I don't remember my first glass—my parents were a permissive sort, and always celebrated with champagne, which meant that I was handed a glass well before I was legal. For my Sweet 16, which was just a party at my house, I somehow convinced my parents to buy me two cases of champagne. We drank it all, and nearly everyone threw up. What a party!

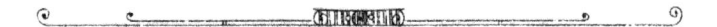

Nowadays, I have two children under three, and a glass of wine after everyone is asleep is one of my great joys. However, sometimes there is no wine...only a bottle of Champagne chilling in the fridge, brought over by someone months ago and forgotten about. The Champagne Necessity is when you pop open that bottle even though you're only going to drink a glass or two, and because you shouldn't have to wait for a party to feel those bubbles on your tongue.

Ingredients needed: one bottle of good Champagne, an otherwise empty refrigerator/pantry.

Open bottle.

Pour into a small glass, champagne flutes discouraged.

Drink.

Close eyes.

Experience a moment of bliss.

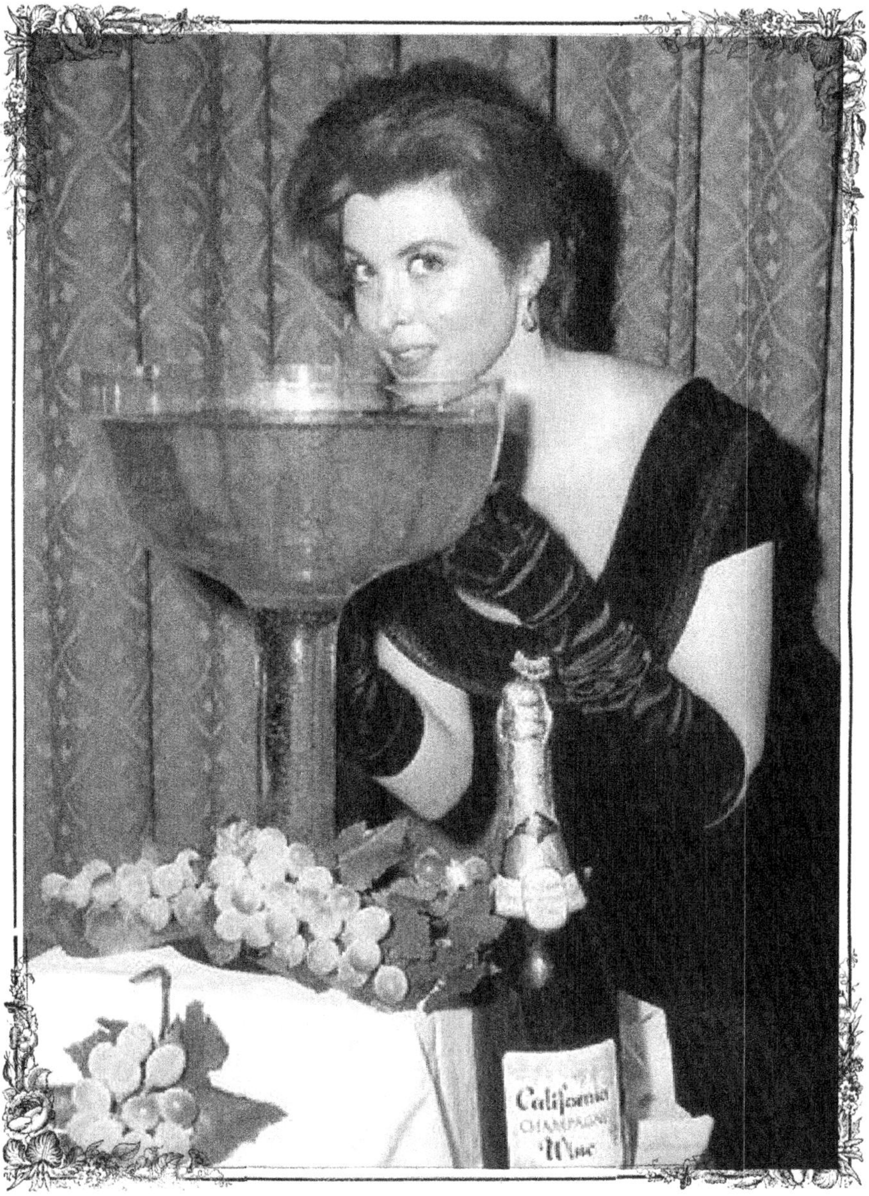
California
CHAMPAGNE
Wine

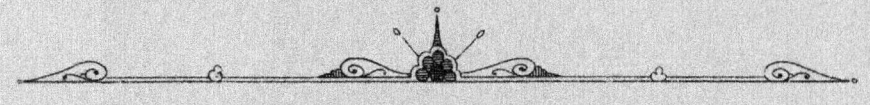

MEGHAN DAUM
A GLASS OF ROSÉ

STEP 1: Be a woman. (Sorry, there's no way around this.)

STEP 2: Have things to discuss with your friends, who are also women. Many, many things. Important things. The specific topics matter less than the almost unbearable sense of urgency you feel about expressing them and hearing what others have to say in response. Think about these topics for weeks while staring at a date on the calendar marked "drinks with K___, J___, and P___." (Acceptable to substitute the initials of the names of your actual friends.)

STEP 3: Arrive at agreed-upon venue. If you live more than half an hour's distance away, arrive early. If you live close, arrive late. Kiss your friends on the cheek, exchange perfunctory compliments about skin or hair or clothing ensemble. Continuing with the perfunctories, take cursory glance at the wine list. You scarcely need to look at it because you already know what you're ordering and there are only one or two options on the menu. You are ordering a glass of rosé. You order the "dryer" one.

STEP 4: Bear in mind, a glass of rosé means two glasses of rosé. If you're not driving, it might mean three glasses of rosé. If this were any other kind of alcoholic beverage, including any other kind of wine, three or even two glasses might seem excessive. But rosé isn't an alcoholic beverage as much as a kind of sports drink for the sport of female conversation. It is the dew that gathers upon the blades of laughter, of gossip, of the ritualized call-and-response that is girl talk. You take a few sips and suddenly the liquid is gone. You order another and it's like grabbing an extra piece of gum on your way out the door. That pinkness confers such innocence, even nothingness! Like the fruity schnapps drinks you downed in college, rosé doesn't take itself seriously, so why should you?

STEP 5: Lose track of how much rosé you've had. Lose count the way you lose count doing "the hundred" in your Pilates class. Feel guilty about this but not too guilty, because, hey, it really doesn't matter. To get drunk on rosé is kind of like having sex without going all the way. It is the "everything but" of inebriation experiences, which is to say you're every bit as likely to feel sick the next day as you'd be if you were drunk on high proof Kentucky bourbon but somehow there's something less shameful about it, something less premeditated, something more akin to being at a wedding where your glass is being perpetually refilled through no fault of your own. That these are bogus excuses is beside the point.

STEP 6: Vow to never, ever drink rosé again because there's something about it that, well . . . there's just something about it.

STEP 7: Repeat steps from beginning.

A.S. KING
RED MIMOSA

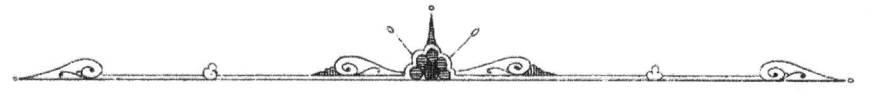

FAVORITE COCKTAIL: Since drinking before lunch hour seems subversive and badass, I've chosen my tweak on the classic Mimosa, which is what I call the Red Mimosa. I've always loved the taste of cranberry juice and orange juice together—but add some bubbles and a nice big breakfast and it's suddenly okay to drink in the morning. Who can argue with this?

FIRST TIME: I was feeling especially daring during a Christmas past. We'd planned Mimosas, but I had some cranberry juice in the fridge. And behind that bottle of cranberry juice lived a very naughty gnome. I am also very naughty so we got along great. He said, "Hey, Amy! Go on! Try adding this! What have you got to lose, love?" So, the short answer to this question is: I had it first around Christmastime because I have a questionable gnome living in my fridge.

Prosecco (You can use Champagne, but it gives me a headache and Prosecco doesn't.)

Orange juice

Cranberry juice

Mix the orange and cranberry juices in even proportions. Then mix half and half Prosecco and the juice mix.

Serve cold in fancy vintage champagne flutes.

BEST COCKTAIL CHATTER: Small talk vexes me. Talk to me about the school-to-prison pipeline and how the downfall of students living in unavoidable poverty is lining the pockets of rich men who can't wait for innocent children to fail. Too heavy for you? Then just crank some good music and I'll start dancing.

FOOLPROOF HANGOVER CURE: Sleep all day.

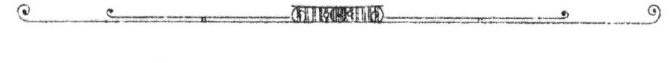

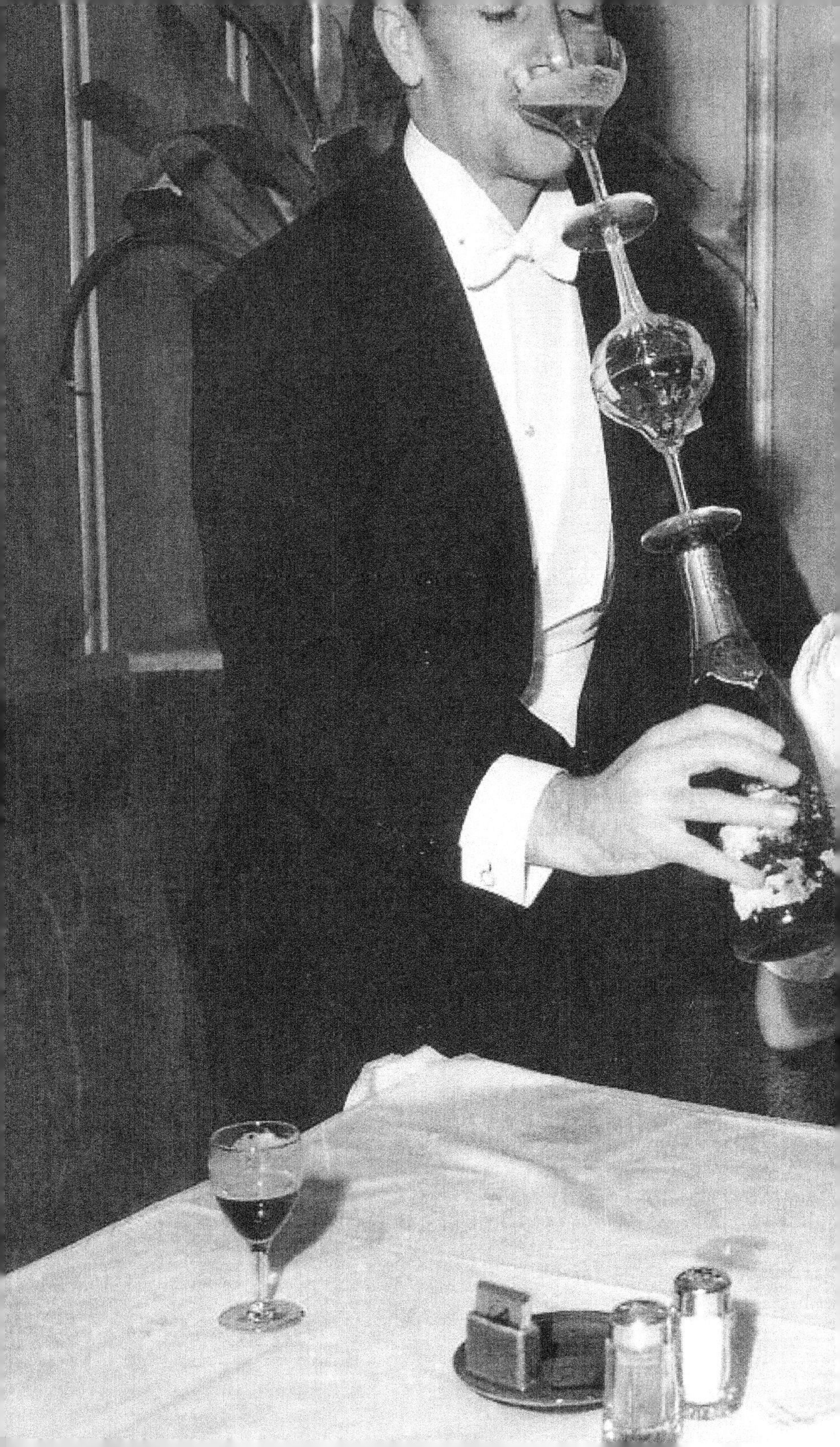

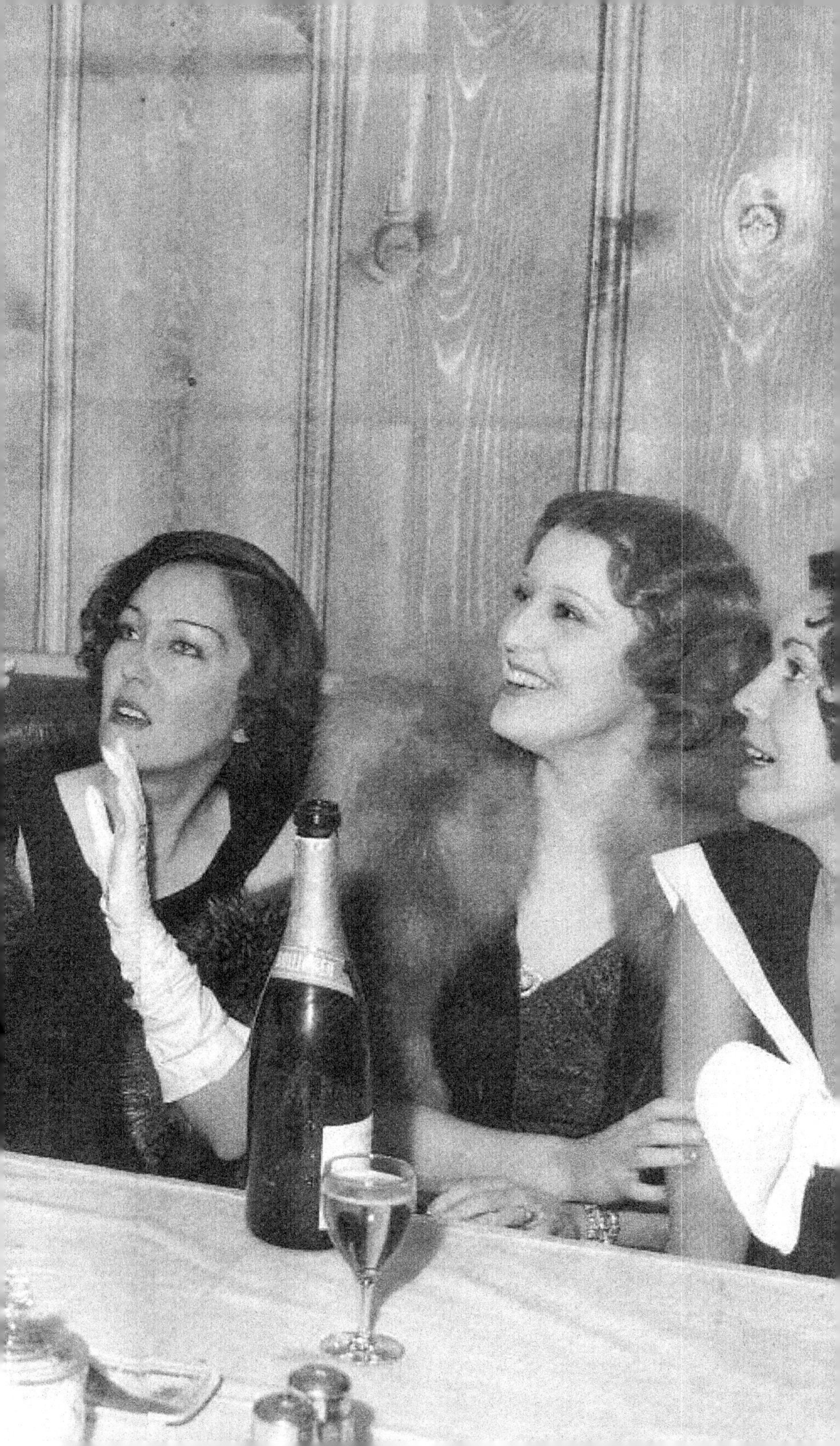

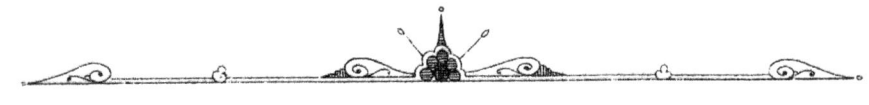

WENDY MASS
SWEDISH FISH & SKITTLES SANGRIA

FAVORITE COCKTAIL: Swedish Fish & Skittles Sangria! The perfect mix of sweet and dry, bubbly and fruity. It reminds me of the days when you're old enough to realize you can buy your own candy and alcohol and can do with it what you please.

FIRST TIME: This drink was invented in college, in the middle of the night—isn't that combination when our most creative ideas were born? It was post-Halloween and my roommate and I had lots of candy and a bottle of cheap Champaign that she'd stolen from her ex-boyfriend's dorm room after he broke up with her through a note scribbled on the dry-erase board on our door. That's the modern equivalent of being dumped via text message! One thing led to another, and voila, The Swedish Fish & Skittles Sangria was born! (Perhaps this invention sparked the idea for my book, *The Candymakers*, although none of the candies entered in the big candymaking contest had alcohol in them!) I've fine-tuned this recipe over the years, but it's a lovely (and colorful!) way to ring in the summer (or any time you need to be reminded that adulthood comes with huge amounts of responsibilities, but also the freedom to be silly and spontaneous and to treat yourself occasionally with something yummy).

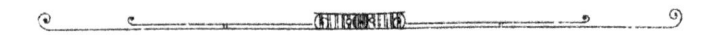

1 bag Swedish Fish (we used only red, but mixed is swell, too)

1 bag Skittles (whatever size you're feeling at the time, or substitute with your favorite soft-ish candy, like Candy Corn)

1 bottle cheap Champaign or any dry, crisp white sparkling wine (if you don't have sparkling wine, just combine the wine with seltzer, or use one of those funky Soda Stream gadgets if ya got one)

2 sliced peaches

2 sliced Granny Smith apples

Any other fruit that you have on hand—like grapes, berries, oranges, or pineapple (apparently sangria aficionados claim you're supposed to use one citrus-type fruit and one non, but any port in a storm)

Mix ingredients in a bowl or wide-topped pitcher, stir very well, and chill for a few hours. Occupy yourself during the wait by going over the reasons why your ex wasn't worth your time. Ladle into glasses, serve with a candy-impaled swizzle stick. You'll soon learn what proportion of candy to fruit to wine you'll prefer and adjust accordingly. Enjoy!

PS. If you want to experiment more with candy drinks, you can make your own shot glasses by melting candy into these very cool silicon shot glass molds. (Just google them, you'll find 'em.)

BEST COCKTAIL CHATTER:
The meaning of life. This was college, after all!

FOOLPROOF HANGOVER CURE:
Yes, just eat the candy and skip the alcohol.

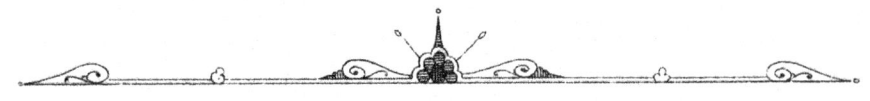

DAVID SWINSON
SPANISH SHANDY

FAVORITE COCKTAIL: I'm a simple guy. I like good single malt Scotch, and fine red wine. But I do love a shandy. It's not so much my favorite drink, just the most memorable. It's a summer drink, and one I will often have during those hot and humid months because it brings me back.

FIRST TIME: I grew up in a foreign service family. When I was a young teenager, we lived in Stockholm, Sweden, for a few years. They didn't have an American Community School there, so my older sister and I had the choice between Frankfurt, Germany, and Mallorca, Spain. As young teenagers, our choice was obvious.

Mallorca.

It didn't take long for me to settle in and make a couple of good friends. On the weekends, we'd take a cab to Palma De Mallorca and explore. One day we stumbled into a small tavern called El Mirador. There was a large mural on the back wall of Alice sitting with the caterpillar on a mushroom and smoking a hookah. Age didn't matter at that time, especially in Mallorca. It didn't take long for us to make friends with the bartender. I wasn't into liquor back then and neither were my friends. Just beer. The bartender asked if we had ever tried a shandy. When he told us what it was it didn't sound like something I'd like, but I tried it anyway, and loved it. I think maybe the bartender didn't think we could handle a whole bottle of beer. Doesn't matter because all we drank when we were there were shandys. Trust me, we spent a lot of time at El Mirador.

Lager beer with orange soda (preferably Fanta), mixed half and half.

BEST COCKTAIL CHATTER: Family. Books. Food.

FOOLPROOF HANGOVER CURE: Hangover? What the hell is a hangover?

Garnishes

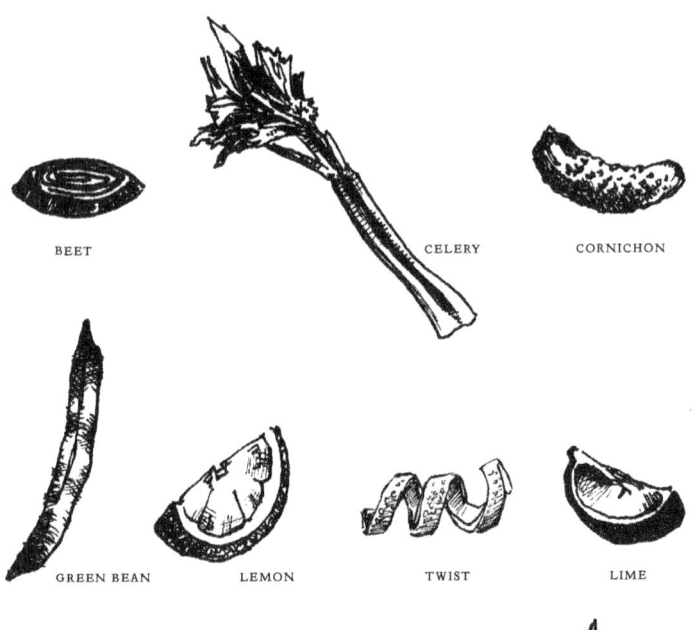

- BEET
- CELERY
- CORNICHON
- GREEN BEAN
- LEMON
- TWIST
- LIME
- MARASCHINO CHERRY
- OLIVE
- PICKLED ASPARAGUS
- TOOTHPICK
- PEARL ONION
- PINEAPPLE

MOCKTAILS

ANTHONY MARRA
STRAWBERRY-BALSAMIC SHRUB

FAVORITE COCKTAIL: I don't drink alcohol, so I usually end up with the most mild-mannered order at the bar ("Your finest soda water, please!"). To pep up the Pellegrino, my cousin-in-law introduced me to shrubs, which are vinegar-based fruit syrups that taste much better than they sound. My favorite is strawberry-balsamic.

FIRST TIME: My cousin and her husband, Gina and Kevin Correnti, own and operate Trattoria Contadina, a fantastic Italian restaurant and fixture in San Francisco's North Beach for over thirty years. Kevin is particularly well known for his cocktails (in an odd quirk of fate, his newest Negroni recipe and my newest book were reviewed in the same pages of the local paper). Over the years, he's fixed me a wide variety of mocktails, and those featuring his homemade shrubs have been among my favorite.

Adapted from The Washington Post's *"Strawberry-Balsamic Shrub"*

Combine in a large Tupperware:

2 cups chopped strawberries

2 cups balsamic vinegar

1 cup sugar

a handful of basil or mint leaves.

Give it all a good stir and leave it to soak in the fridge for a week. Then strain the mixture into a bottle and add to your favorite glass of soda water or cocktail.

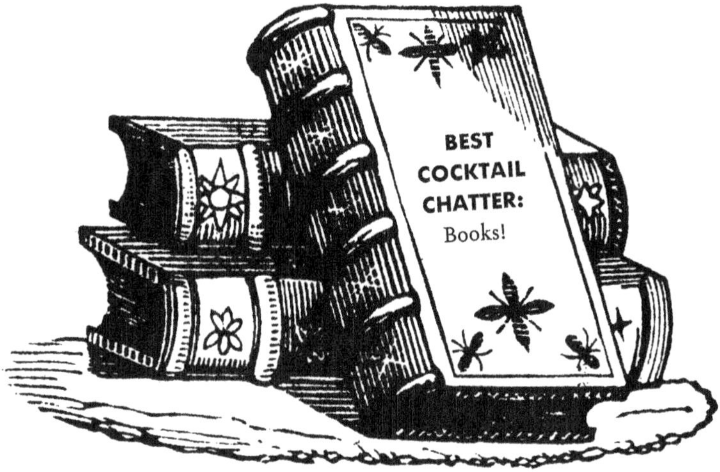
BEST
COCKTAIL
CHATTER:
Books!

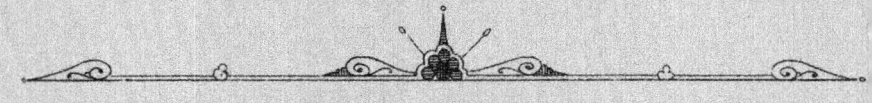

NOVELLA CARPENTER
BEET KVASS

FAVORITE COCKTAIL: Well, I stopped drinking, so I'd have to say beet kvass.

FIRST TIME: At some hippie fermentation festival. I think Sandor Katz was even there, as a judge for the best-tasting fermented beverage. There was kombucha, of course, and some god-awful whey-based bubbly drinks, and then there was the beet kvass. It had the texture of blood, the color of beets (duh), and the sparkle of something special. It tasted like something only family members should share.

Yank some beets out of the garden.

Wash them off (sorta).

Cut up in big hunks.

Place beet hunks in a glass jar, cover with water and 1 tsp of salt per beet.

Cover with a cloth to prevent bugs from falling in and let sit for one week on the kitchen counter.

After a week, decant the liquid off the beets (eat the beets if you want).

Drink neat.

BEST COCKTAIL CHATTER: Urban farming, of course.

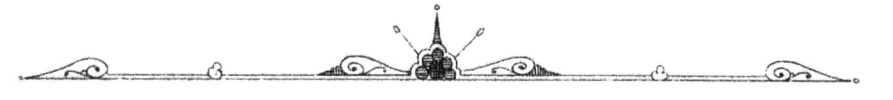

BILL CLEGG
HOT GINGER, HONEY & LEMON TODDY

FAVORITE MOCKTAIL: (I drink without alcohol but you can add as little or as much bourbon as you like)

FIRST TIME: When I was studying in Scotland my junior year in college, I once had a terrible cold and a bartender at the pub closest to campus set me up. It's great on a winter night and has magical powers over chest and head colds.

Boil water and fill a teapot with half a lemon cut into quarters and seeded. Squeeze juice into the pot first and drop the quarter slices in after. Add 1/8th of a cup of freshly chopped ginger (small chunks but not mush) and let steep for at least five minutes. Pour into mug and stir in a tablespoon of raw honey and with the other half of lemon squeeze a little extra fresh juice. Drink!

BEST COCKTAIL CHATTER: Books!

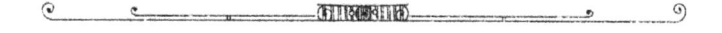

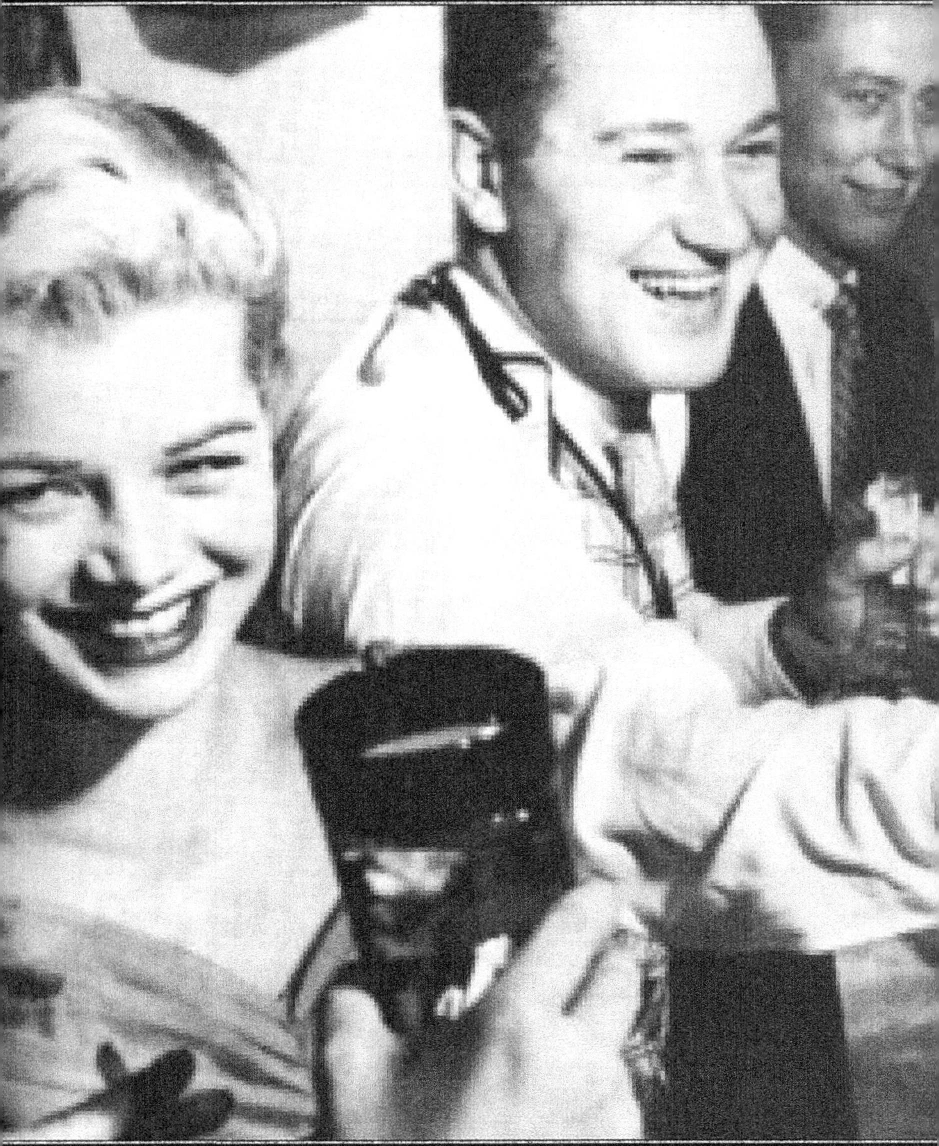

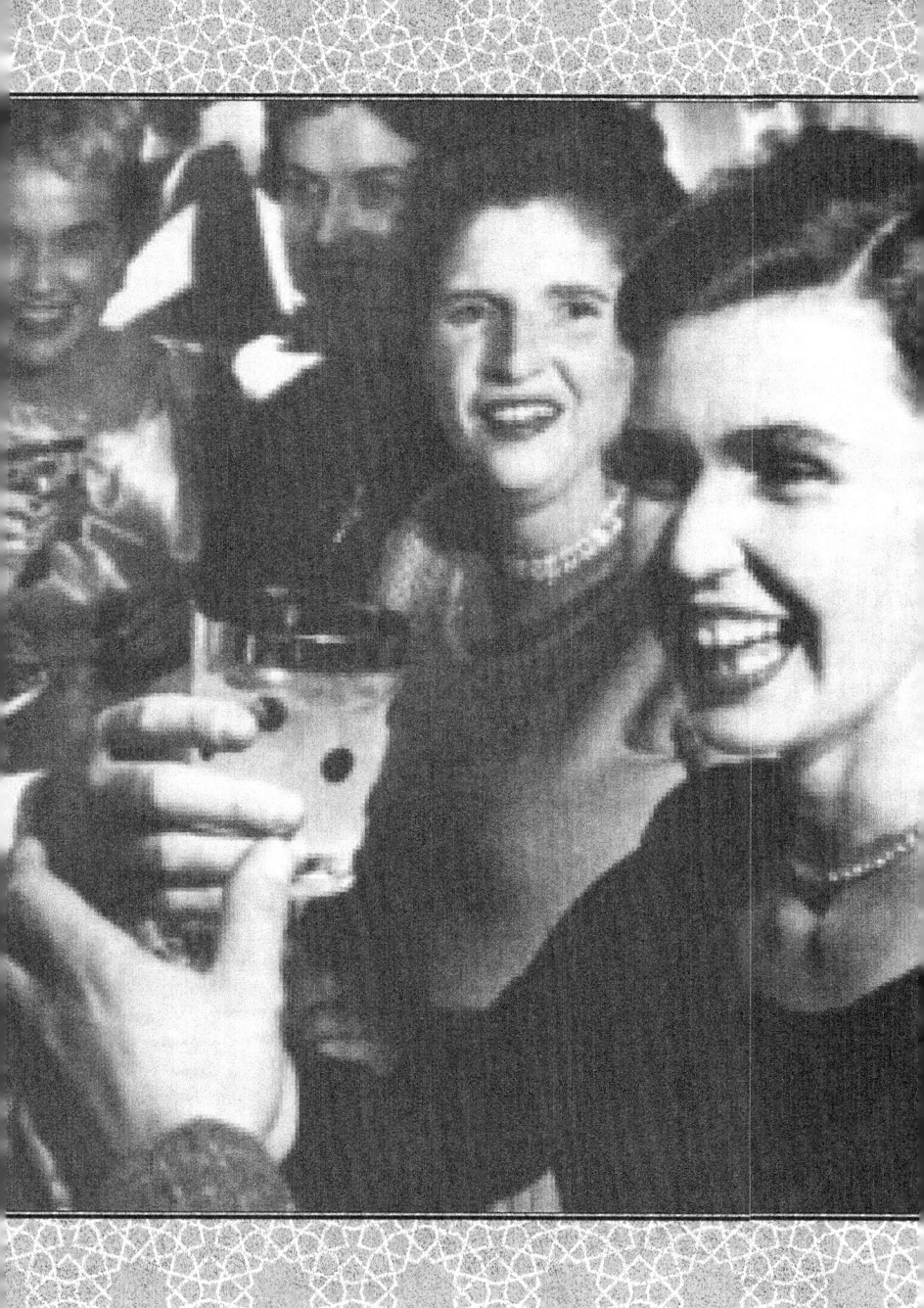

CONTRIBUTORS

KAREN ABBOTT is *The New York Times* best-selling author of *Sin in the Second City*, *American Rose*, and, most recently, *Liar Temptress Soldier Spy*, named one of the best books of 2014 by *Library Journal*, the *Christian Science Monitor*, Amazon, and optioned by Sony for a miniseries. A native of Philadelphia, she now lives in New York City, where she's at work on her next book.

In the words of *The New York Times*, **LOUIS BAYARD** "reinvigorates historical fiction, rendering the 19th century as if he'd witnessed it firsthand." Bayard's eight novels include the Edgar-nominated *The Pale Blue Eye*, *The New York Times* Notable *Mr. Timothy*, and the recent *Lucky Strikes*, named one of the best young-adult titles of 2016 by Amazon. His other novels include *The Black Tower*, *The School of Night*, and *Roosevelt's Beast*. He is also a nationally recognized essayist and critic whose articles have appeared in the *Times*, the *Post*, the *Los Angeles Times*, *Salon*, and *Bookforum*.

NOVELLA CARPENTER is an urban farmer in Oakland, California. She teaches farming and writing at University of San Francisco. Her books include *Farm City: The Education of an Urban Farmer* and *Gone Feral: Tracking My Dad Through the Wild*.

BILL CLEGG is the author of the memoirs *Portrait of an Addict as a Young Man* and *Ninety Days*, as well as the novel, *Did You Ever Have a Family*.

SLOANE CROSLEY is the author of *The New York Times* best-selling essay collections, *I Was Told There'd Be Cake* and *How Did You Get This Number*, and the novel *The Clasp*. *I Was Told There'd Be Cake* was a finalist for The Thurber Prize for American Humor. She has been a frequent contributor to *The New York Times*, *The Village Voice*, *The New York Observer*, and is currently a contributing editor at *Vanity Fair* and *Interview Magazine*. She serves on the board of Housingworks Used Bookstore and is a co-chair of The Young Lions Committee at The New York Public Library.

MEGHAN DAUM is the author of four books, most recently *The Unspeakable: And Other Subjects of Discussion*, which won the 2015 PEN Center USA Award for creative nonfiction. She is also the editor of *The New York Times* best seller *Selfish, Shallow & Self-Absorbed: Sixteen Writers on the Decision Not To Have Kids*. Her other books include the essay collection *My Misspent Youth*, the novel *The Quality of Life Report*, and *Life Would Be Perfect If I Lived In That House*, a memoir. Since 2005, Meghan has been an opinion columnist at the *Los Angeles Times*, covering cultural and political topics. She is the recipient of a 2015 Guggenheim Fellowship and a 2016 National Endowment for the Arts fellowship and is an adjunct associate professor in the MFA Writing Program at Columbia University's School of the Arts.

JULIA GLASS is the author of *Three Junes*, winner of the 2002 National Book Award for Fiction; *The Whole World Over*; *I See You Everywhere*; *The Widower's Tale*; and *And the Dark Sacred Night*. A recipient of fellowships from the National Endowment for the Arts, the New York Foundation for the Arts, and the Radcliffe Institute for Advanced Study, Glass also teaches fiction writing, most frequently at the Fine Arts Work Center in Provincetown. She lives with her family in Marblehead, Massachusetts.

LAUREN GROFF is the *New York Times* best-selling author of three novels, *The*

Monsters of Templeton, Arcadia, and *Fates and Furies,* and the celebrated short-story collection *Delicate Edible Birds.* Her work has been featured in *The New Yorker, Harper's, The Atlantic,* and several *Best American Short Stories* anthologies; has won the Paul Bowles Prize for Fiction, the PEN/O. Henry Award, and the Pushcart Prize; and has been a finalist for the National Book Award, the National Book Critics Circle Award, the Orange Award for New Writers, and the *Los Angeles Times* Book Prize. She lives in Gainesville, Florida with her family.

DANIEL HANDLER has published many books under his own name, including *The Basic Eight, We Are Pirates,* and *Adverbs,* and many books under the name Lemony Snicket, including *All the Wrong Questions,* the picture book *13 Words,* and the best-selling *A Series of Unfortunate Events,* which debuted as a Netflix series in 2017. He lives in his native San Francisco with his wife, illustrator Lisa Brown, and their son.

HOMER HICKAM is the author of many books including his acclaimed memoir *Rocket Boys.* His awards include the University of Alabama's Clarence Cason Award for Nonfiction and Shepherd University's Appalachian Heritage Author's Award for his memoir trilogy set in the coalfields of West Virginia. His latest novel is *Carrying Albert Home: The Somewhat True Story of a Man, his Wife, and her Alligator.* Homer, his wife, and their cats split their time between homes in Huntsville, Alabama, and St. John of the U.S. Virgin Islands.

JOSHILYN JACKSON is the *New York Times* best-selling author of six novels, most recently *The Opposite of Everyone.* She lives in Decatur, Georgia, with her husband and their two kids.

A.S. KING has been called "One of the best YA writers working today" by *The New York Times Book Review.* She is the author of highly-acclaimed YA/crossover novels including *Still Life with Tornado, I Crawl Through It,* the 2012 *Los Angeles Times* Book Prize winner *Ask the Passengers,* 2011 Michael L. Printz Honor Book *Please Ignore Vera Dietz,* among others. After fifteen years living self-sufficiently and teaching literacy to adults in Ireland, she now lives in Pennsylvania with her weird family.

MIN JIN LEE's debut novel, *Free Food for Millionaires* was a Top 10 Novels of the Year for *The Times* (London), NPR's *Fresh Air,* and *USA Today.* Her short fiction has been featured on NPR's *Selected Shorts* and *One Story.* Her writings have appeared in *Condé Nast Traveler, The Times* (London), *Vogue, Travel+Leisure,* the *Wall Street Journal,* and *Food & Wine.* Her essays and literary criticism have been anthologized widely. She served as a columnist for the *Chosun Ilbo,* the leading paper of South Korea. From 2007-2011, she lived in Tokyo where she researched and wrote *Pachinko.* She lives in New York with her family.

EDAN LEPUCKI is the author of the novella *If You're Not Yet Like Me* and the novel *California.* Her new novel, *Woman No. 17,* will be published in May 2017. Edan is a graduate of Oberlin College and the University of Iowa Writers' Workshop. She is a contributing editor to *The Millions* and the founder of Writing Workshops Los Angeles.

SAMUEL LIGON is the author of two novels— *Among the Dead and Dreaming* and *Safe in Heaven Dead*—and two collections of stories— *Wonderland,* illustrated by Stephen Knezovich, and *Drift and Swerve.* His short fiction has appeared in *Prairie Schooner, New England Review, New Ohio Review, Gulf Coast,* and *Okey-Panky,* among other places, and his essays appear in *The Inlander.* Ligon edits the journal *Willow Springs,* teaches at Eastern Washington University in Spokane, Washington and is the artistic director of the Port Townsend Writers' Conference.

BETH LISICK, author of *The New York Times* best sellers *Everybody into the Pool* and *Helping Me Help Myself* is also a performer and an odd-jobs enthusiast. She has contributed to public radio's *This American Life* and is the cofounder of the monthly Porchlight storytelling series in San Francisco. A Bay Area native she now lives in Brooklyn, New York.

JACQUELINE LUCKETT is the author of the novels *Passing Love* and *Searching for Tina Turner*, and the essay "Traveling with Ghosts," included in *Best Women's Travel Writing 2011*. Luckett received her Masters in Fine Arts in Screenwriting from the University of California Riverside in 2015. The Bay Area native lives in Oakland, California, and continues her travels to nurture her passion for photography and exotic foods.

ANTHONY MARRA is the author of *A Constellation of Vital Phenomena*, which won the National Book Critics Circle's inaugural John Leonard Prize, and appeared on over twenty year-end lists. Marra's novel was a National Book Award long list selection as well as a finalist for the Dayton Literary Peace Prize and France's Prix Medicis. His story collection, *The Tsar of Love and Techno*, was a National Indie Bestseller and an NPR's First Read. He received an MFA from the Iowa Writers' Workshop and was a Stegner Fellow at Stanford University, where he now teaches. He has lived and studied in Eastern Europe, and now resides in Oakland, California.

WENDY MASS is *The New York Times* bestselling author of *The Candymakers* series and nineteen other novels for young readers. They include *A Mango-Shaped Space, Jeremy Fink and the Meaning of Life* (which was made into a feature film), *Every Soul a Star,* and the *Willow Falls* series that began with *11 Birthdays*. Her latest is a series for beginning readers called *Space Taxi*. She is working on her next book while building a labyrinth in her backyard. Not at the same time, of course. That'd be weird. She and her family live in the wilds of New Jersey. wendymass.com.

VIET THANH NGUYEN's novel *The Sympathizer* is a *New York Times* best seller and won the Pulitzer Prize for Fiction. Other honors include the Dayton Literary Peace Prize, the Edgar Award for Best First Novel from the Mystery Writers of America, the Andrew Carnegie Medal for Excellence in Fiction from the American Library Association, the First Novel Prize from the Center for Fiction, a Gold Medal in First Fiction from the California Book Awards, and the Asian/Pacific American Literature Award from the Asian/Pacific American Librarian Association. His other books are *Nothing Ever Dies: Vietnam and the Memory of War* (a finalist for the National Book Award in nonfiction) and *Race and Resistance: Literature and Politics in Asian America*. He teaches at the University of Southern California. His short story collection, *The Refugees,* was published in February 2017.

BRAD PARKS is the only author to have won the Shamus, Nero, and Lefty Awards, three of crime fiction's most prestigious prizes. His first standalone thriller, *Say Nothing*, released in March, 2017 from Dutton Books in the U.S., along with thirteen other publishers worldwide. Parks's six previous novels chart the adventures of sometimes-dashing investigative newspaper reporter Carter Ross, and have collectively won stars from every major pre-publication review outlet. A graduate of Dartmouth College, Parks is a former journalist with *The Washington Post* and *The Star-Ledger* (Newark, N.J.). He is now a full-time novelist living in Virginia with his wife and two school-aged children.

JAMES PATTERSON has had more *New York Times* best sellers than any other writer, ever, according to *Guinness World Records*. Since his first novel won the Edgar Award in 1977 James Patterson's books have sold more than 300 million copies. He is the author of the Alex Cross novels, the most popular detective series of the past twenty-five years, including *Kiss the Girls* and *Along Came a Spider*. He writes full-time and lives in Florida with his family.

MOLLY PRENTISS was born in Santa Cruz, California, in 1984. She has been a Writer in Residence at The Blue Mountain Center, Vermont Studio Center, and at the Workspace program at the Lower Manhattan Cultural Council, and received the Emerging Writer Fellowship from the Aspen Institute. She holds an MFA in Creative Writing from the California College of the Arts. *Tuesday Nights in 1980* is her first novel. She currently lives, writes and walks around in Brooklyn, New York.

KATE SCHATZ is the author of *The New York Times* best-selling books *Rad Women Worldwide* and *Rad American Women A-Z*, as well as the 33⅓ book *Rid of Me: A Story*. She's the co-founder of Solidarity Sundays, a progressive feminist activist group. She lives in the San Francisco Bay Area with her kids, her dude, her pets, and her cocktails.

AMY STEWART is the co-owner of Eureka Books in Eureka, CA. She's also the author of eight books, including *The Drunken Botanist: The Plants That Create the World's Great Drinks*. Her new novels, *Girl Waits with Gun* and *Lady Cop Makes Trouble*, are the first in a series based on a true story.

EMMA STRAUB is from New York City. She is the *New York Times* best-selling author of the novels *Modern Lovers*, *The Vacationers*, and *Laura Lamont's Life in Pictures*, and the short story collection *Other People We Married*. Her fiction and nonfiction have been published in *Vogue*, *New York Magazine*, *Tin House*, *The New York Times*, *Good Housekeeping*, and *The Paris Review Daily*. She is a contributing writer to *Rookie*. Straub lives with her husband and two sons in Brooklyn, New York. She is the 2017 Independent Bookstore Day Author Ambassador.

DAVID SWINSON is a retired police detective who served 16 years with the Washington DC Metropolitan Police Department. He is the author of *The Second Girl* and *Crime Song*. *The Second Girl* was one of *The New York Times'* and Booklists' best crime fiction books of 2016. Swinson currently lives in Northern Virginia with his wife, daughter, bullmastiff, and Staffordshire terrier.

AMOR TOWLES was raised in a suburb of Boston, Massachusetts. He graduated from Yale College and received an M.A. in English from Stanford University where he was a Scowcroft Fellow. His novel, *Rules of Civility*, reached the best seller lists of *The New York Times*, the *Boston Globe*, and *Los Angeles Times* and was rated by *The Wall Street Journal* as one of the ten best works of fiction in 2011. It has been published in 15 languages; the French translation received the 2012 Prix Fitzgerald. His most recent novel is *A Gentleman in Moscow*. He lives in Manhattan with his wife and two children.

Born and raised in Reno, Nevada, **WILLY VLAUTIN** started playing guitar and writing songs as a teenager. It was a Paul Kelly song, based on Raymond Carver's *Too Much Water So Close to Home*, that inspired him to start writing stories. Vlautin has published four novels: *The Motel Life*, *Northline*, *Lean on Pete*, and *The Free*. He founded the band Richmond Fontaine in 1994. Driven by Vlautin's dark, story-like songwriting, the band has achieved critical acclaim at home and across Europe. Vlautin currently resides in Scappoose, Oregon.

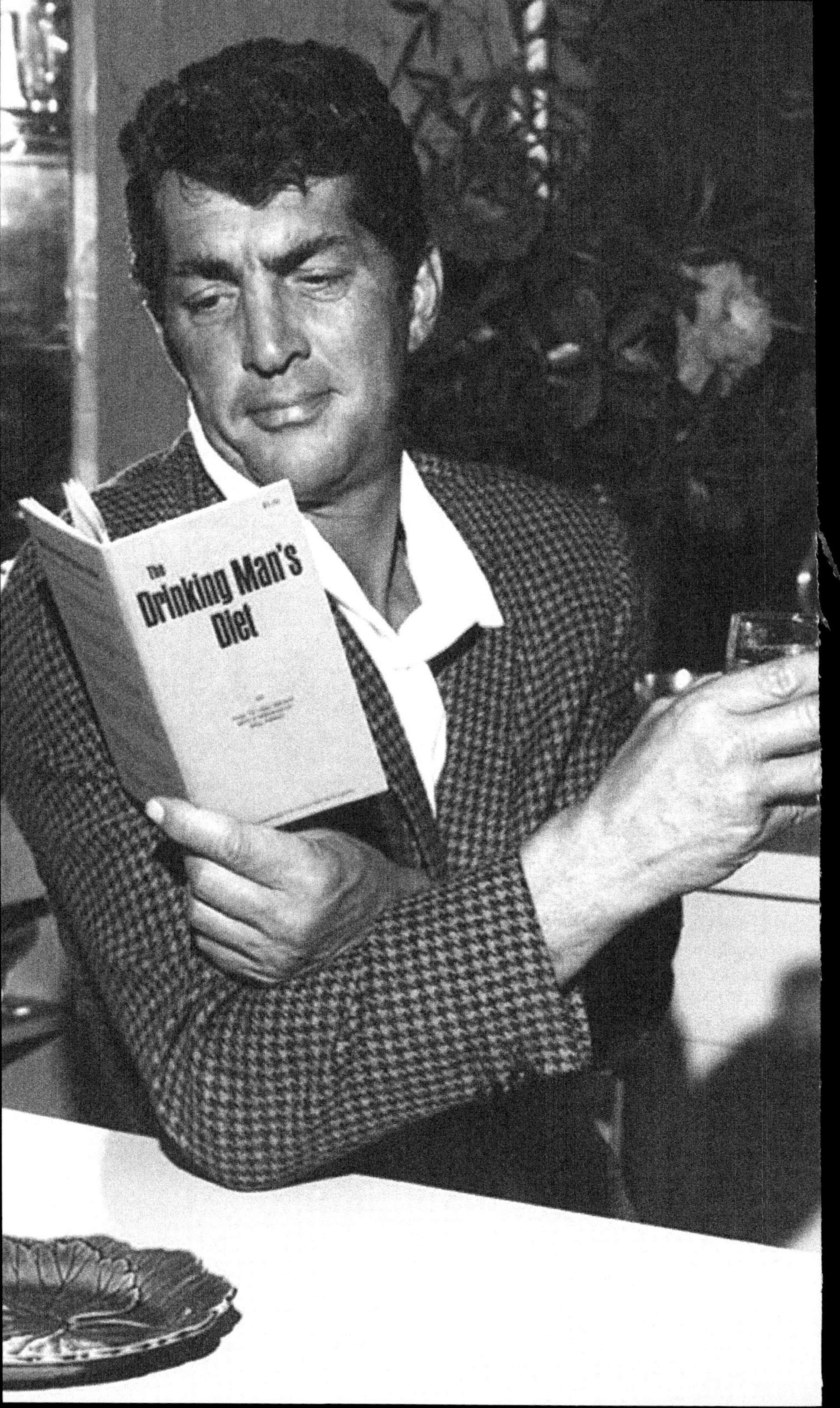
The
Drinking Man's
Diet

CPSIA information can be obtained
at www.ICGtesting.com
Printed in the USA
LVOW03*1930150317
527355LV00004B/6/P

9 780998 449913